Writing the Dead

Figurae

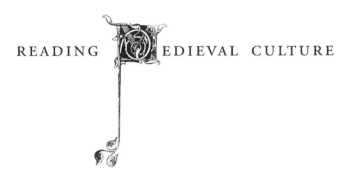

READING MEDIEVAL CULTURE

Writing the Dead

Death and Writing Strategies
in the Western Tradition

Armando Petrucci

Translated by Michael Sullivan

Stanford University Press, Stanford, California, 1998

Writing the Dead:
Death and Writing Strategies in the Western Tradition
was originally published in Italian in 1995 under the title
Le scritture ultime: Ideologia della morte
e strategie dello scrivere nella tradizione occidentale.
© Giulio Einaudi editore s.p.a.

Published with the assistance of the Getty Grant Program

Stanford University Press
Stanford, California
© 1998 by the Board of Trustees of the
Leland Stanford Junior University

Printed in the United States of America

CIP data appear at the end of the book

Contents

Contents viii

Illustrations

Illustrations follow p. 60.

Preface

One could write the history of mankind with the help of tombs.
　　　　　　　　　　　　　　　　　　　　—Viollet-Le-Duc

In 1964, Erwin Panofsky began his essay on funerary sculpture with a confession of inadequacy in the face of the vast theme he had chosen: "An art historian," he stated, "can approach the subject of these lectures only with the greatest trepidation. Trespassing on the preserves of many adjacent disciplines . . . he has to rely largely on secondary sources and often finds himself confronted with a diversity of opinions, at times about crucial points, that he, a rank outsider, cannot presume to evaluate." Panofsky's caveat of more than thirty years ago may also—*si parva licet componere magnis*—be applied to this essay. It necessarily has to range over the vast span of time, embracing practically the whole history of Western humanity, and find its way through extraordinarily diverse areas of culture, historical experiences, and accumulations of evidence. What made the conception and the writing of it possible was the unitary nature of the source in question, the written funerary witness and the usages adopted in its creation, practiced in unbroken fashion from the first millennium B.C. down to the present.

　　This work would not have been possible without the support and help of various great libraries in which I have had the good fortune to work in recent years: the library of the American Academy and the Biblioteca Hertziana in Rome, the Biblioteca Apostolica Vaticana, the Biblioteca della Scuola Normale Superiore in Pisa, and the Newberry Library in Chicago. The text has benefited from the suggestions and expert knowledge of many friends and colleagues, whom I here thank warmly, but do not name, since it would be impossible to record them all. Let me at least mention Guglielmo Cavallo, Vittorio Dini, Raffaele

Giampietro, Luigi Moretti, who is sadly no longer with us, Paola Supino Martini, and Carlo Tedeschi. My wife, Franca Nardelli, has reread the whole book and furnished many useful suggestions.

～～

This book does not pretend to examine the boundless literature devoted by human culture to the theme of death. Its aim, instead, is to sketch out the set of writing practices and written products employed to record the dead in a public way. It was my view that a history of this activity and its manifold products would be particularly useful for an understanding of the purposes and social categories of the peoples among whom these practices began, the ways in which they developed, how they changed over time, the people they involved and interested, where they were set up, and the weight they had in the written cultures of the Western tradition.

We well know the importance for the constitution of the earliest human cultures of the modes, means, and rituals of what Jean-Pierre Vernant has felicitously called "the politics of death that every social group must institute and administer in continuity according to its own rules if it is to establish itself with its own specific features and have its own structures and goals endure over time." It is my conviction that the introduction and the use of writing constituted and constitute an element of great importance in the definition of the "politics of death" proper to the cultural traditions I have set myself to examine.

So although this book has practically no chronological limits, it has a very clear one in the cultural and geographical area chosen, largely, Mediterranean civilization, Europe, and North America. Nowadays, such a choice might be thought conservative and illegitimate by some, perhaps even by many scholars, and I am fully aware of the fact. It seemed unavoidable, however, if I was not to overstep the limits of expertise of which I spoke at the start and keep to a terrain that enjoys, if nothing else, a substantially unitary tradition of study and a wealth of organically constituted written sources.

In recent decades, the subject matter of death has been a central theme in European historiography, especially in the French language or those dependent on it, and it is amply represented in the sources of which I have made use. But from what emerged during my preparatory research, nobody has yet looked at the problematic nexus constituted by the relationship between the dead and writing or at the usage—

introduced at a certain point and never abandoned—of making a written record of the dead in determined ways and places.

It was not my intention to write a continuous history of this relationship and usage over time. Such a project probably would have been
impossible, or its outcome would have been too much of a compila-
tion. I have preferred on the one hand to keep to expository discourse—largely within a chronological framework, from prehistoric
antiquity to our own day—and on the other to highlight certain situations or certain themes along the way that bring out moments of crisis
or change in the practices of writing employed in a coherent strategy of
funerary record.

The sources chosen for the thesis offered here consist, at least in theory,
of all the possible types of testimony broadly commemorative of the
dead in which writing was used. In the majority of cases, these are testimonials intended for public display and hence consist of epigraphical
material. But as written commemorations of the dead, they can just as
well consist of scrolls, books, manuscripts, or loose printed matter,
newspapers, and posters.

The choice of samples was dictated by the topic under discussion,
with a prevalence sometimes of epigraphical material, sometimes of
book evidence, or of a variety of other items. Nevertheless, it was always a matter of a series, or sometimes of segments, of isolated pieces
of evidence gathered in the course of personal research, rather than of
an organic tradition of studies, something practically nonexistent in
this specific field. According to the situation, samples chosen on the
basis of what may be described as "fieldwork"—that is, research con-
ducted personally in churches, cemeteries, museums, and in the man-
uscript collections of libraries—yield place to others derived mainly
from the existing bibliographical *corpora* as, for example, with the written culture of the classical age.

Within the limits of the possible, the evidence was sifted to establish its material characteristics, focusing on the elements relating to the
graphic style and quality of the writing employed, the modes of
arrangement and layout of the text, the link between the written text
and the pictorial elements (for example, the likeness of the deceased),
the extent of the text, the techniques employed in execution, the number of people involved in the making of the testimonial, its outward

aspect, its form and format. It should hence be clear that, as with my earlier research on the public testimonial, this inquiry concentrates on the external and material aspect of written productions, rather than on the matter of the text and its content, and that this has led me to base my investigation on originals or on photographic reproductions and to leave aside collections of texts, especially epigraphic ones, merely reproduced as print.

Apart from the analytical schema to which every exemplar was subjected, the inquiry set itself certain basic problems worth outlining here, since they provide a further and less external interpretive map of the work done and its meaning.

As Michel Vovelle has said, "there is nothing more unequal than death." The first problem I had to face was that of trying to make out what proportion of the dead had a right to a "written death" in any period and what differences existed from this point of view from age to age and from culture to culture. This has meant indicating all the obvious links with the greater or lesser extent of literacy, with forms of government and the organization of power, with the distribution of wealth, and with the demographic variables that it was possible to identify. Over the extremely long span of time considered, periods with a widespread right to "written death," such as fifth-century B.C. democratic Athens or early Christianity, have been followed by periods and situations, such as the archaic age or the early Middle Ages, when there was a dramatic reduction in the use of writing the dead. There also have been differences within the same period, for example, between different provinces of the Roman Empire or between Protestant and Catholic culture in modern Europe. In each of these cases, the funerary use of writing turns out to be strictly linked to the underlying causes of the dominant social culture, to the forms of government, and to the unequal spread of written culture. No aspect of it is coincidental or indifferent.

I already have said that the funerary use of writing is an important element in the "politics of death" every organized culture sets up and administers so that it may stand out as itself. However, another principal problem I sometimes have to leave unanswered concerns the identity of those (priests, intellectuals, politicians) who in any given situation designed the modes for funerary writing, decided on formulas and models, oversaw the material execution, and founded textual and artistic traditions. It is they who have been responsible over time for the variety of postures adopted by written productions commemorating the dead, the general and in particular the graphic aspect of ancient necropolises, Christian catacombs, modern cemeteries, obituaries, and death notices. From their capacities or cultural weaknesses has come the shaping force that the writing of death has exerted on the whole of the written culture of a particular period, or on its marginal subordination to that culture. It is they who were responsible for the way and degree to which the ideology of death, on which every organized society is based, was transfused into the forms of public writing.

Moreover, public writing is, by definition, addressed to a public. To whom? Ever since writing began to be put on tombs—perhaps in the fourteenth century B.C. in the Egypt of the Eighteenth Dynasty— it has been done so that what was written would be read by someone: but by whom? That, too, is a query that lends itself to different answers according to the situation. If at the start, in ancient Egyptian culture, funerary writing mainly was addressed to the gods and to the dead, in democratic Athens, it was addressed to the citizens; and in Christian culture, to the community of the brethren in Christ, but also to God; and then, in the Middle Ages and in modern Europe, to someone and to nobody at the same time, to a potential public both real and false; and today, to a fragmented and indifferent society that recognizes itself only in the atomized relationships of restricted family nuclei within which the written message of death has to perform its minimal function.

One of the underlying features of the funerary use of writing in every period is its relationship to the body of the dead, for, as we know, there can be commemorative writings linked to the remains ("in praesentia") and hence set where they are laid, that is, on the tomb, and analogous writings placed elsewhere, far from the remains ("in absentia"), but aimed equally at recording the dead. The strategies adopted in the placing of funerary writings are neither a matter of chance nor a matter of indifference to the historian. They are determined, and in their turn determine certain fundamental aspects of the ideology of death, such as the division of land between the living and the dead, the degree of respect owed them, their greater or lesser visibility, and even, from a more general point of view, the presence or not of a historical and commemorative record in a given society—in short, the birth of historiography itself.

All these aspects and problems can, in fact, be compressed into the single, fundamental inquiry underlying this study: what has been the function of the funerary uses of writing over time? Leaving aside the question of how, why did people begin to "write" certain of their dead and gradually extend the custom to practically all their dead?

I must make clear immediately that the reasons why people began to deal in any way with dead bodies—by burial, cremation, endocannibalism, and so on—never had any relationship with the reason why at a certain moment they began to attach writing to mark and identify burial grounds. The practices whereby dead bodies were dealt with and administered arose largely as practices of defense adopted by the society of the living toward the society of the dead and as ritual homage to the dead, aimed at warding off and distancing its power and its feared capacity for action. By contrast, in the vast majority of cases, the apposition of writings on funerary deposits is a practice of the living addressed to other living beings. It is a substantially and profoundly "political" practice aimed at celebrating and recording the power and social presence of the group, corporate or familial, to which the deceased belonged and is directed at consolidating its wealth, prestige, endurance over time, vitality, and capacity for reproduction and expansion.

From this standpoint, the use of writing to record and celebrate the dead brings together some of the great strands in the cultural history of humanity: the relationship of the living to the dead, the cohesion and endurance of the genus, the right to individuality, control of land, the formation and administration of power, mechanisms for the maintenance of wealth, and the symbolic and signifying value of written culture. If all this is true, what is given here is not so much a history of the dead and of deaths as a history, exactly like all the other possible histories, of the living and of life, shaped by pride and exclusion, domination and ideology, fear and cruelty, affections and memories.

Writing the Dead

The Tomb and Its Signs

Shaped by the sword into simulacra of man, green over the graves, the cedars tower from afar as guardians of the memory of illustrious mortals; and gnarled by the seasons, their trunks descend among pitted marbles, where on the shapeless bust of the hero are sculpted images of wild beasts and plants, which singly and together are charged with manifold sequences of ideas that hand on his name, his conquests, the laws he gave to the fatherland, the worship he set up to the gods, his exploits, times, sayings, and the apotheosis that brought him into the chorus of the blessed: thus, the first altars to the immortals were burial grounds.

The words come from a speech by Ugo Foscolo. In 1809, three years after the writing of *I sepolcri*, this was how he saw the modes and forms of the earliest burial places and rhetorically depicted them for himself and others. We can now draw a more exact and detailed picture of the first phases of this typically human activity. We know now that many tens of thousands of years ago, between 70,000 and 35,000 B.C., prompted by feelings of a religious nature and by reverential awe, Neanderthal man began to bury at least some of his dead in neighboring graves, at times leaving offerings and gifts. We also know that later, in the course of the early Paleolithic period (between 35,000 and 8,500 B.C.), funerary customs became more frequent and complex, and that sometimes the burial places were marked with stones or a red ocher that was also used to tinge some corpses. We believe that all this represented an enormous advance in man's capacity for reasoning and abstraction, that evidently it was then that he began to conceive strategies to control and ward off the grievous event that struck directly at the family structure to which he belonged and that menaced his own life. In this very distant period, we believe, the bases of funerary practices that were to last through the few millennia of our better-known history were first set up, and the culture of the Neanderthals, and of the *homines sapientes sapientes* who succeeded them, already had posed fundamental problems concerning the inviolability, durability, and recording of burial places and also had found answers, no doubt inadequate and fragile, but within certain limits wholly functional and rational. We are convinced that these peoples managed to conceive a relationship with death such that the dead continued some form of life in a world apart, different from that of the living, and that a set territory would be reserved for them where they might remain apart from the world of the living without disturbing intrusions; that it was necessary to keep them in their world; and that this could be done by making offerings to their needs and by penning them in their allotted place by enclosures and coverings that were more than symbolic.

This led to marking the places of the dead with piles of stones, large single stones, visible enclosures, and so on, while any eventual record of single burials, that is, of the individual dead, probably remained entrusted to memory and oral transmission within the group concerned.

When the shift took place in the course of the Neolithic period from a system of more or less organized graves to tomb systems proper, the problem of marking funerary deposits to ensure the separation of the dead from the living and of the practices of offerings from the living to the dead arose in more concrete and complex ways. In this period, as we know, a system of production based on agriculture and stock breeding was developed, the first urban settlements were established, and society became structured in classes and categories according to rank and functions. It was precisely then, between the Neolithic period and the Bronze Age, that in differing civilizations and in diverse regions of Europe, Asia, and Africa, systems were adopted for marking *certain* tombs (not all) with high tumuli of earth and stones, *dolmen* tombs were built for whole clans and used over several generations, and the great circular *tholos* tombs were constructed in Mycenae for the kings. In these cases, the wish to mark the burial places of the dead went along with the desire to distinguish the places of some dead from those of others. Thus, the message carried by the sign became more complex and no longer addressed the few directly concerned—

members of the same family, of the same nucleus, the administrators of the same funerary space—but was aimed at society as a whole.

~~~~

2.   Over the period spanning the second and third millennia, two of the Mediterranean civilizations involved in this phenomenon of publicly distinguishing certain tombs, the Egyptians and Minoan-Mycenaeans, knew and adopted writing as a system of recording words, names, and concepts, but they made very different uses of it. Whereas in Egypt, writing was employed, even if within a closed and rigidly hierarchical social structure, on a variety of materials and for differentiated functions, from documentation to the making of books, from the epigraphic to the ordinary, what is known as "Linear B" was used in the Minoan-Mycenaean world only within the royal palace as purely and simply a system of administrative recording. It was natural, therefore, that the first—and for a long time, the only—civilization to adopt writing for funerary purposes and in burial contexts was the Egyptian.

From the time of the first dynasties (3100 B.C. onward) the Egyptian civilization worked out a complex ideology of death, at the center of which were the concept of the survival of the dead and the conservation of their individual identity. Besides ensuring these two main goals, the burial system had in some way to reproduce the complex and rigid hierarchy that ruled and stratified society, marking off funerary deposits according to the rank the dead had belonged to in life.

Generally speaking, the Egyptian ideology of death was addressed to the future life of the dead within the kingdom of the dead to which they belonged, and even the funerary activities of the living were in some way exclusively addressed to the afterlife, not to this world. From this standpoint, writing performed a double function. The first and most important was that of succoring the future life of the dead person and was thus addressed to the deceased himself and to the gods, and so was used exclusively within the tomb. The second, much more modest function, was external, and addressed to the public who were to ensure the survival of the dead through offerings. This is why the facade of individual tombs had a false door—in the Middle Kingdom, transformed into a true stele. Besides various images and a likeness of the dead, it bore a more or less extended and more or less formulaic text giving the name of the dead and proclaiming the need of funerary offerings if his "Ka" were to survive. The case of an administrator of property, a certain Simentwoser (Eleventh Dynasty, 2134–1191 B.C.), is interesting. He makes a first-person address directly to the public and gives a summary of his career, setting forth his merits and asking that his memory be allowed to live on.

The obsession with identity and the identification of the dead was such that further writing with the dead man's name and attributes was placed on the sarcophagus and sometimes directly on the body, but even in these cases, the context is that of communication with the world of the beyond, not with that of the living. Moreover, since, as I have said, one of the primary purposes of the burial system was to safeguard the corpse and the dead person's "Ka," the funerary signs, both figured and written, addressed their message more to the inside than the outside world. And in various ways, the attempt was made to conceal the tomb and make it impossible to find, even in cases like those of the royal pyramids, where the casing was a building of enormous proportions and highly visible.

Elsewhere, in northern Europe, in Africa, in the Near East, the burial places of kings and nobles were indicated by large markers of earth or stones: tumuli, menhirs, large stelae, some of them figured, all symbolic means of occupation and delimitation of the land, but with no element to identify the dead and, above all, devoid of writing.

In the Mesopotamian world, though writing served specific functions in society, the written funerary inscription never appeared. Only rarely do written signs appear—within the tombs, never on the outside—as a means of identifying and of accompanying the dead. As with the Egyptians, in the Mesopotamian civilizations, the use of external writing clashed with the desire to conceal the burial place and safeguard the bodies of the dead and their grave goods, and was therefore not adopted.

From the Sign to the Text

1.   The *Iliad* is a great poem of death, and in it, the dead, funerals, and tombs are strongly present. A stele is often mentioned next to or above the tomb; indeed, the honor given to the dead is precisely rendered in the formula "with tomb and stele":

> and there brothers and companion will pay honor
> with mound and stone, for this is the honor of the dead.
> (*Iliad* 16.456–57)

The stele is described as an upright, fixed slab on which one can lean:

> as a gravestone stands unmoving set on the grave mound
> of a man or a woman who has died. . . .
> (*Iliad* 17.434)

> leaning on the stone, next to the tomb
> raised to Ilos, son of Dardanos. . . .
> (*Iliad* 11.371–72)

The stele as an element marking the tomb reoccurs in the *Odyssey*, and with it appears a further sign, an oar, to mark and distinguish the tomb of the sailor Elpenor:

> And as the dead man was burned, and the weapons of the dead man,
> the mound raised, a stone erected above,
> we planted on top of the mound the handy oar.
> (*Odyssey* 12.13–15)

But for two of the most important tombs in the epic of Troy, that of Patroclus (*Iliad* 23.245–48) and that of Hector (*Iliad* 24.795–801) there is no mention of a stone, but only a large, high tumulus. In the warrior and mythical society of which the Homeric poems are the imaginative reevocation at a remove of a great many centuries, the stele was thus an important element in the burial, along with the tall and visible tumulus, already a recognizable sign in itself, both *sēma* and *mnēma*.

What the Homeric poems say, however, may be referred with due care more to Greek eighth-century society—of which they were a direct product—than to mythical Mycenaean culture. Alphabetical writing had existed in Greece for some time by then, perhaps for a century, and certainly was employed, even if neither the *Iliad* nor the *Odyssey*, later by some decades, make mention of written stones, perhaps to avoid an anachronism that might have appeared too blatant to its hearers.

It is clear that for the Greek aristocratic society taking form in the city, the figure of the young fallen warrior who populates the *Iliad* constituted an important element in the identification and celebration both of the stock and of the city to which they belonged. Burial within the walls, rather than outside was arranged for them, and a complex system of signs of identification and of personal celebration was developed that made the individual tombs of the heroic dead into testimonials bearing clear messages that spoke to all. A system of communication came into being that for the first time addressed not so much the dead man himself, or the gods of the Underworld, but the living, a system that served the living and that had been devised for them, in their language, and for their altogether human and political purposes.

2.   According to Jean-Pierre Vernant "the erection of a tumulus crowned by an upright stone or by a planted wooden post marked the desire to inscribe the presence of the dead on the surface of the ground, too, and to mark it out to the living forever."

For a long time in the Greek world, funerary stelae were to transmit their messages through decoration, images, and symbolic allusions. Then, toward the end of the seventh century, the pressing need for the personal identification of the dead, for perpetuation of his person and his name, led to the intrusion of the likeness and of writing into a space previously given over to a purely abstract and generic discourse, and with them came a new range of meanings, the possibility of a dialogue with the reader, and the participation of kinfolk, who were also recorded and sometimes spoke. Thus, throughout Greece, but particularly in Attica, the stele began to change into a communal focus precisely because it had become freighted with a strong social meaning.

In the nascent aristocratic "polis," the recording of the dead—at first only the hero, then, gradually, many other dead, and hypothetically, all the dead—became a process of shared identification that had high political significance. Writing and image constituted basic and decisive elements in this.

First came the names, bare and unadorned, then the texts. The earliest surviving examples of inscribed stelae come from the necropolis of Sellàda on the Calchidean island of Thera (Santorino) and date from the eighth century. These include one dedicated to a certain Eteocleia, whose name, written downward, occupies the whole space, while the lettering is reversed. Also from Sellàda comes a block of lava, the face and three sides of which are covered with the names of nine men—presumably killed in the same skirmish—arranged in irregularly boustrophedonic fashion, with the two end lines curving upward. Again from Thera comes a clay model of a painted house bearing an inscription vertically arranged on two small side columns. On the burial stele of Praxilas, from the same locality and of the same period, the writing is laid out in the form of a curved cornice. On Corcyra, the great tumulus of Menecrates, proxenos of the city, dating from the last quarter of the seventh century, has an inscription, a long text in hexameters in memory and celebration of the dead, stretching ten meters around the base.

Very soon, in fact, texts more or less short included the name of the dead man along with either the circumstances of his death or the name of the person responsible for commissioning the tomb. Thus, one of the earliest surviving stele bases, found in Corinth and probably dating from the early seventh century, has a short text of three irregularly parallel lines recording that Deinias died in a storm. Another inscription dating from the first half of the seventh century, found on Amorgo in the Cyclades, has a debatable text running from right to left in two oddly curving lines recording that a father Pigmas erected the funerary monument of Deidamas. In analogous fashion, in Athens itself, the base of a stele from the second half of the seventh century records that it was shared by a father and daughter, Enialo and Keramos. The text, written from the left, is also laid out in two parallel curved lines.

A boustrophedonic inscription, irregular in layout and alignment and dating from the late seventh century or the early sixth, records in two first-person hexameters that a father, Eumares, having built the tomb (*sēma*) to his son Androcles, erected the stele to be his memory (*mnēma*). The short verse text expresses extremely clearly the complex meaning and duality of the message that tomb and stele by then had taken on in common awareness, a message the writing embodied as it explicated it.

3.   The earliest complete stele (dating perhaps from 600 or 600–575 B.C.) comes from Tanagra and is dedicated to Dermis and Kittilos, two young brothers who probably died together in battle. It shows them nude, standing side by side above a base on which the dedicatory hexameter is carved in irregular fashion. We have here for the first time an arrangement of writing rationally separated from the sculpted figure, even though the alignment is not geometrical. By contrast, a tall pillar erected in Trezene around the mid-sixth century B.C., or not much later, bears three lines, two running upward and one downward, consisting of three epic hexameters in Homeric style, which state that Ison erected the monument to Praxiteles, but that it was his companions who heaped the tumulus in one day.

In short, during the sixth century B.C. and into the first half of the fifth century, while the need to identify the dead through writing and commemorate them in a text (often in verse) spread wider and wider in archaic and aristocratic Greece—probably through the direct influence of epic culture—no organic and unitary system had yet been found for a rational division of the funerary stele between text and image or for arranging the sometimes long and complex text in an ordered and clearly readable way. And it was precisely because of Greek influence that analogous tendencies and analogous problems arose, even in the funerary epigraphy of other Mediterranean areas and of archaic Italy, first in the Greek colonies, then among the native peoples themselves.

From sixth-century pre-Hellenic Lemnos, for example, comes a mysterious funerary stele of a warrior (Holaie), in which the writing (similar to Etruscan) is placed in three differing areas of the empty space around the effigy, in a chaotic upward, downward, and boustrophedonic layout. In Sicily, a Syracusan stele with vertically arranged text records a certain Alexis; from Selinunte, again in the first half of the sixth century B.C., come two stelae written boustrophedonically. The Etruscan world has left a certain number of stelae with images of standing warriors on which the inscription runs in semicircular fashion, stripwise on the cornice. The Volterra stele of the warrior Avile Tite, dating from 550 to 530 B.C., in which the writing runs along the edge, is a classic example. In other cases—such as the well-known Warrior of Capestrano, dating from the late fifth century B.C.—the writing is arranged upward on the small column supporting the statue or is carved upward in serpentine fashion in a way that makes a reading entirely problematic.

Like the earlier Greek examples, these, too, show that archaic models of layout that did not favor reading survived into the sixth and even the fifth century B.C. throughout the entire Mediterranean, models deriving from a culture of the sign, rather than a culture of lettered communication through writing. All of them were destined to be replaced sooner or later by a new graphic norm that was to become common, first to the Hellenistic and then the Roman imperial heartland.

The Order of the Text

1. A new norm for the disposition of displayed script arose and took hold in Athens in the second half of the fifth century B.C. under the tyranny of Pisistratus and later of his sons, Hippias and Hipparcus.

This norm involved a sharp differentiation between the writing area and the area for images in funerary stelae and entailed a series of important choices in terms of layout and the arrangement of the text of an inscription. These brought in horizontal linearity, shown—at least in the earliest period of the reform—in the ruling of lines; a single direction for the writing, from left to right; layout in horizontal lines one above the next; a narrow cut; and spacing between letter and letter, rather than between word and word. Almost all of these options were then to remain the unchanging patrimony of exhibited writing for millennia, indeed, right down to today, and very probably were taken over from the model of book writing, in which horizontal line arrangement, right-to-left progression, the regular sequence of the lines in columns, and a uniform and basically thin stroke were obvious necessities within a container like the book volume in scroll form. It is worth remembering that tradition attributes the first "edition" proper of the Homeric poems to Pisistratus himself, and furthermore that the graphic layout of the most ancient Greek literary papyrus that has come down to us, the *Persae* of Timotheus, dating from the fourth century B.C., is very close to that of the epigraphs of the archaic period.

Whether or not one accepts the notion that archaic Athenian epigraphy was modeled on the "book" (i.e., took over the column arrangement of the scroll, the book of the period), the fact remains that the process of normalization and homogenization that it then underwent, particularly in funerary inscriptions, obviously was aimed at ensuring an immediate and fluent reading of the text that the obvious technical and practical hindrances of earlier arrangements—vertical, spiral, boustrophedonic, or in any case, not ordered according to a single norm—militated against.

In a certain sense, then, it was in the aristocratic, but wealthy, powerful, dynamic, and open Athens of the period of Pisistratus that the written message marking a burial place was for the first time laid out so as to favor its reading by the eventual urban public to which it was clearly addressed.

The rise and application of the new norm can be easily seen in a series of examples of Athenian funerary monuments that cannot be dated more exactly than as being of the age of Pisistratus.

The writing on the base of a (lost) stele (dating from 560–550 B.C.) dedicated to Teticos, killed in battle, is still boustrophedonic and un-ruled, but perfectly aligned in six lines and carved with a thin stroke, while the text makes clear epic references. The contemporary two-line epitaph given to Chairedemos, which also bears the signature of the sculptor Phaidimos, is ruled, instead.

Four stelae, slightly later and belonging to the middle years of the tyranny, demonstrate the graphic normalization in its full application. One is dedicated to Pythagoras, proxenos of Selimbria in Thrace, and the writing is placed in two different areas of the epigraphic space, the bare indication of the name above, and the epigram proper laid out in four lines on the base (indeed, on the upper segment of it), perfect in its simple, graphic elegance. The second is the truly splendid stele dedicated by their father to a young brother and sister, Filo and Megakles. Topped by a sphinx (and thus earlier than ca. 530 B.C.) and dominated by a representation of the pair standing in profile, the inscription on the base is arranged in two ruled lines that could not be better laid out or more readily legible. In analogous fashion, the inscription on the base of the stele of the young Kroisos, killed in battle and portrayed nude, walking, dating from after 520 B.C., is ruled and normalized, while the inscription on the stele of Aristion, another warrior hero, the work of Aristokles, restricts itself to the name set out on the base, as in the other examples, and dates from the last decade of the fifth century B.C.

Outside the Athens of Pisistratus, the new norm spread slowly and unevenly. It shaped the inscription of the splendid statue of Phrasikleia—the work of Aristion of Paros—found at Myrrinos in Attica.

The text, laid out in five unruled lines, is not perfectly regular in alignment. The text of the fragmentary stele of Agathon and Aristokrates of Thespis is aligned much worse, while the layout of the inscription on the burial stele of Charonidas of Rhodes, probably from the early fifth century B.C., is chaotic and unruled, even if aligned. In analogous fashion, the layout of funerary inscriptions in Sicily is again irregular, while the fifth-century stele of Archeos of Melos, written in large, imperfectly homogeneous letters, but ruled with large grooves obviously of purely ornamental value, is quite out of the ordinary.

2.   Fifth-century democratic Athens inherited the deployment of exhibited writing as readable message from the aristocratic and tyrannical city of the previous century, but extended its use to the full inside and outside the city and brought the legibility of epigraphic texts to a peak.

Pausanias tells us that Athens had sanctuaries of the gods and tombs of heroes and of men outside the city, in the parishes, and along the roads. The monumental cemetery of the Cerameicus he describes still held inscribed tombs, shared and individual, of heroes and illustrious citizens from the earliest period—though some had been removed as building material for the construction of Themistocles' wall in 480–479 B.C.—down to the age of Pericles and beyond. Before reporting Pericles' funeral oration for those who fell during the first year of the Peloponnesian War (431), Thucydides also records that the fallen were buried with public honors in the Cerameicus, the finest suburb of the city.

It is undoubtedly true that during the whole of the fifth century and down to the early years of the fourth century B.C., Athens produced a very high number of inscriptions, certainly a very much greater number than was produced during the previous century. It is also clear that the passage from tyranny to the democratic regime must have led to a notable extension (in no way quantifiable) of the right to "written death" to strata of the population until then excluded from a practice largely reserved for aristocratic families.

Domenico Musti has pointed out that epigraphical production was characterized during the democratic period by order, clarity, structure, legibility, durability, and terse lucidity—in short, by a "rational use of writing." As we have seen, there already had been a certain shift in the direction of normalization of funerary epigraphy in the age of the tyrants, but it is beyond debate that during the age of Pericles, this tendency widened into a geometric regularizing of writing and into a systemization of previously neglected graphic spaces. According to Stanley Morison, "there are four primary characteristics of early Greek letter design in the classical period. First, the apparent squareness of the shapes; secondly, the uniformity of the stroke; thirdly, the consistency of the complete structure; lastly, the rationality of the shapes as having no unnecessary part and nothing superfluous. Thus, the script is square, uniform, rational and perfectly functional." In Athenian funerary stelae from the fifth and early fourth centuries, the geometrization of writing and the structured division of space between text and image reached levels of balance and graphic expressivity hard to match. The outcome was a very high degree of particularization and celebration of the dead in which image and text performed their separate tasks in an autonomous and yet reciprocal way.

3.   Thanks to the layout and a skillful disposition of sometimes very large areas of empty space, the emphasis given to the writing is very strong, even in cases (the majority) where the text is reduced to the essential minimum, just the name or a very brief phrase of dedication. A few examples from the abundant and substantially uniform production should suffice. The stele of Eupheros, for instance, shows him standing in profile with a strigil in his hand, and just his name, lightly carved and gracefully spaced, on the upper edge of the frieze. It is the case also in the numerous stelae of young, seated women shown alone or with offerers, once (the stele of Eutamia) even with a dog, of which that of young Egheso is perhaps the finest. It is also true of the splendid well-known stele of the young castaway Democleides, seated in the prow of a ship, where the name stands out sharply on the cornice of the frieze.

In other examples, by contrast, the text is more complex and consists of an epigram proper. One very well-known example is that of Ampharete, portrayed seated with a small grandson in her arms, where two verses are inscribed on the cornice above the name, set apart on the upper edge of the frieze. Probably the most famous funerary stele from Athens, however, is that of Dexileos, a casualty of the Corinthian War of 394–393 B.C. A unique case, the text, arranged in four lines of perfectly geometric and rigidly laid-out script, records the birth and death dates of the twenty-year-old hero. The city also dedicated a stele—of which we have fragments—to those who fell in the same war. It shows a battle scene (analogous to that on the stele of Dexileos), followed by a perfectly ordered list of the fallen.

The geometrical order of the epigraphic text shows itself in all its complex clarity in the stelae where lists of war dead are divided by tribes. They lack any kind of image, any superfluous frieze. The clarity and the legibility of the closely written lists, set side by side in columns and clearly based on a book model, rely entirely on the graphic composition of space, on a variety of sizes, sometimes larger, sometimes smaller, on the perfect squaring of the letters, on the uniformity of the signs, and on the contrasting layout of list and epigrammatic text, all of which make the latter, carved on the base in lines that run the full width of the base, stand out strikingly.

In single stelae, however, an excess of writing was considered improper. In the *Laws*, Plato declared that tumuli should not be too high and inscriptions should not go beyond four epic verses, enough to contain the elegy for the dead. Nevertheless, the greater complexity of exhibited writing—in terms of name and epigram—between the fifth and fourth centuries leads one to believe that the process of inscription was phased in time and spread over several stages, not least because sometimes the two epigraphs look carved by different hands. It also leads one to think that there was a willingness to turn the writing to a more complex purpose, not only that of record and celebration, but also of exorcism of the dire happening. Only slightly later, however, Hellenistic gigantism (the mausoleum of Mausolos at Halicarnassus, for example), followed by the application in Athens of the sumptuary laws of Demetrius Phalereus (317–315 B.C.), decreed the end of Attic funerary writing and its terse and sober style of expression. In 200 B.C., during the invasion of Philip V of Macedonia, many of the stelae in the Cerameicus were destroyed.

The Order of Memory

I.

> Cornelius Lucius Scipio Barbatus, son of Gnaeus,
> was a strong and wise man and endowed with every virtue;
> he was consul, censor, aedile amongst you. Taurasia and Cisauna
> in Samnite country he took; he subjugated the whole of Lucania and
> brought back hostages.

The great tomb of the Scipios, dug into the tufa along the Appian Way, opened the history of the relationship between the dead and writing in Rome. Among the various sarcophagi placed there, that of Lucius Scipio Barbatus, consul in 298 B.C. and founder of the family, is the only one that has come down to us intact and is the most famous of them. It bears a double inscription, the earlier and original one painted in minium, the second, in Saturnian verses and dating from the early second century B.C., added when the use of the *elogium* had become established in republican Rome, at the time when a moderate spread of literacy, an autochthonous written (and literary) culture, and a consequent political use of writing were coming into being.

The pride of the "Cornelian clan," its wish to distinguish itself in death as in life and in the memory of posterity, is evident even in the choice of inhumation, rather than cremation, which was by then customary in Rome, where it was to remain so well into the imperial age. According to Pliny the Elder: "cremation among the Romans was not of old standing: they used to bury in the earth." The use of the sarcophagus made available several writing surfaces, useful when it was decided that the memorial text could not and should not be restricted to the name inscribed on the lid, but be transformed into a true commemorative composition, an *elogium* that was also a history. In the Barbatus tomb, the two functions of praise and record merge into a single sequence. In the later one of Gnaeus Scipio Hispanus, praetor in 139 B.C., the text with details of his career is arranged in three lines, separately from the elegy proper, which consists of two graphically different elegiac couplets perhaps added later. In both these illustrious examples of commemorative writing, the script is arranged in horizontal lines, with the alignment still uncertain, the division of the lines lacking relationship with the text, and no concern for layout. But it is beyond doubt that during the second century B.C., the Roman senatorial aristocracy conceived its own model of commemorative funerary text in which the ordered succession of public offices, set out according to the so-called *cursus honorum*, or curriculum of honors, came gradually to be seen as fundamental. The tomb of Scipio Hispanus, with its separation between the two sections (inscribed, perhaps, at different times), is a clear example of this, as it is on the formulaic level in its presentation of a model career:

Cn. Cornelius Cn. f. Scipio Hispanus, pr[aetor], aid[ilis], cur[ulis] q[uaestor], tr[ibunus] mil[itum], [decem]vir l[itibus] iudik[andis], [decem]vir sacr[is] fac[iundis].

Gnaeus Cornelius Scipio Hispanus, son of Gnaeus, praetor, curile aedile, quaestor, military tribune, one of the judicial committee of ten, one of the committee of ten for the performance of religious functions.

2.   According to Pliny the Younger, images of the dead console precisely because they proclaim their honor and glory: "For if the images of the dead set up at home relieve our mourning, how much more those by which not just their likeness or face, but also their honor and glory, are reported in a very well known location." It is highly probable that honorary monuments to the living and the dead, in absence of the remains, aimed to replicate the fame of the dead already honored by commemorative tombs. At least that is what one may deduce from another passage in Pliny the Elder, where he speaks explicitly of statues with "the record and honors of men" inscribed on the bases, "nor is so much to be read on tombs."

The great dead, independently of the presence of the body, were to be honored with images and with inscriptions that identified them and recounted their story, deeds, and honors and handed them on to posterity. For this biographical data—or, if you prefer, bureaucratic, unquestionably official information—to achieve its commemorative purpose, it had to display the internal chronological order that exactly defined a "career," a followable, imitable model sanctioned by the state, coincident with the destiny of the "res publica" and with the glories of the family of which the dead had been a member and to which the dedicators of the monument belonged.

Thus, the republican age gave rise to the model of the funerary inscription of a public man. It was arranged biographically according to the stages of his public career, tersely constructed according to a fixed formula of instructional type—rich in allusive abbreviations and readable only by those with the proper skill—that served to compress the text and render it still more dignified in the symbolic complexity of its signs. Like the one erected in the first half of the first century B.C. to the aedile Caius Poplicius Bibulus by a decision of the senate in session (*senato consulto*) "for reason of his honor and virtue," and still standing today in the open air of Piazza Venezia in Rome, they were sometimes set up at the expense of the republic. The text is arranged breadthwise, according to the old Scipionian model, in five lines of almost perfectly squared capitals of a single size. But from the Augustan age onward, the true schema of the bureaucratic-official inscription for the Roman who had filled public offices was to be completely geometrical from the formal point of view. Framed in the raised cornice of the rectangular slab, divided into several lines according to an artful pattern of longer and shorter lines, given visual rhythm by the skillful use of as many as three or four different letter sizes, now larger, now smaller, the funerary inscription of the public man in imperial Rome took on the symbolic value of a model, and, in the persistence of its image over the centuries, is still influential in the epigraphy of modern and contemporary Europe.

Countless examples of this graphic model have come down to us; here, let me mention just a few. The monument erected on Monte Orlando near Gaeta in memory of Lucius Munatius Plancus takes the form of a circular mausoleum with a large inscription on the entrance, laid out in six lines and employing three different sizes of letter, and again dates from the first century, around 20 B.C. The tombstone of Potitus Valerius Messalla, consul suffectus in 29 B.C., dates from a few years later (10–12 A.D.). The marvelously arranged four-line text is a miracle of graphic balance and formulaic distillation. The *cursus honorum* of Agrippina the Elder, wife of Germanicus and grandmother of

Nero, set entirely within mention of her family, is quite singular. The slab is laid out in perfect fashion, with the word "OSSA" looming long and large at the beginning. The tomb inscription of Nymphodotos, freedman and archivist of the imperial household (37–62 A.D.), is the product of a large, skillful Roman workshop. The harmonious relationship between the geometry of the graphic forms and the alternation of three letter sizes, laid out in eleven lines, gives it an absolute graphic clarity.

Later, in the third and fourth centuries A.D., variants and novel elements were inserted in the rigidly repeated model and impaired the graphic norm. This can be seen in the sarcophagus of Sextus Varius Marcellus, father of the emperor Heliogabalus (217–18 A.D.), where elongated capitals fork ornamentally and ivy leaves ("ivy leaves setting apart") function as dividers. Later again, the marble slab of the great senator Vettius Agorius Praetextatus (384–85 A.D.), has a long *cursus honorum* in which his pagan religious career precedes his civil one and takes up as many as 22 lines, with some overlapping on the cornice to the right and with uniform justification on the left.

3.   During the republican and early imperial periods, the language of funerary writing was thus characterized by certain constant elements: the geometrization of the graphic forms; alternation of different sizes to highlight the most significant portions of text (name, specific offices, etc.); layout with alternating lines (now a full line, now a centered line); clear separation between the writing space, usually framed by a raised cornice, and the space (or spaces) given over to images, usually a portrait (or portraits) or a genre scene.

This rigid formal strategy—which also shaped official contemporary epigraphy—matched a complex series of mental attitudes that insisted on the tomb's eternal value and inviolability and on permanence for its funerary writing. Ample space and a central position of maximum visibility were always granted to the latter. However, it was the written text itself that became the carrier of these mental attitudes, claimed inviolability and duration for the monument and the tomb, entrusted its defense to the heirs, and as final precaution, established its measurements and made them known. In Roman legal doctrine, a principle of direct correspondence was established between tomb and funerary inscription. A passage given by Julius Paulus states: "Whoever

cancels the inscribed epitaph . . . is seen to have violated the tomb."
On the other hand, since tombs and the areas lodging them were
"things bound by religion," they were inviolable, and funerary inscriptions also partook of this acknowledged sacrality.

The eternity hoped for and the inviolability sanctioned by the law
was meant not only to ensure the inviolability of the bodies laid in
tombs, but also, if not especially, was aimed at guaranteeing that the
"nomen" of the dead man, his memory, his personality in all its different manifestations, private and public, would endure through time.

Some inscriptions are explicit on the point: "this stone will both
be a safeguard of the tombs after death and will give a judgment on
the dead buried here" (*Corpus inscriptionum latinarum*, 11, 1616), as is
this from the republican period: "This dwelling is eternal, here am I
set, here will I be forever." Others similarly declare: "the stone and the
name alone remain, no trace besides" (*Corpus inscriptionum latinarum*,
6, 22215), or: "the earth holds the body, the name the stone and the air
the soul" (*Corpus inscriptionum latinarum*, 3, 8003). There is also Tri-
malchio's naively explicit testimony about his tomb, devised in such a
way that anyone looking was forced to read his name: "A sundial in
the middle so that whoever wants to look at the time will read my
name, willy-nilly" (Petronius, *Satyricon*, 71, 2).

"Out of this religious nucleus," suggest Angelo Brelich, "the cult
of the *memoria* of the dead developed. The survival of the memory, of
the reputation—which can consist simply in the survival of the
name—was felt by ancient man as a species of immortality." This feeling excluded insertion in an absolute chronological series. Memory,
though rooted in time, did not require an external chronological
marker, and dated tombstones of the classical age are very rare. Inclusion in the relative chronological sequence constituted by the biological
data of genealogy ("son of," "brother of," "wife of," and so on) is on
the other hand always detailed. The passing reader, the chance visitor,
to whom the epigraphic discourse was often enough addressed, was not
required to measure the gap between himself and the dead against a
background of absolute time, but only to accept the opportunity of
knowing and acknowledging him within the chronological segment he
had occupied in life, one that embraced three generations at most: his
own, the one previous to him, the one that followed.

The tight grid of the writing's geometrical structures corresponded,
in short, to a message entirely contained within itself, defined in terse,

formulaic language, and autonomous in its schematic completeness. But this was not always and everywhere the case.

⁓

4. In Roman society, the humble were excluded from the right to written death. On the still-uninhabited Esquiline "the common tomb . . . of the vulgar poor," says Horace in the persona of an obscene wooden Priapus (*Satires*, 1, 8, 10). Between the second and third centuries A.D., the tombs of the humble, void of any written indication, amphorae planted in the soil or simple square monuments covered by tiles, were packed close to the mausoleums of the rich and powerful in the cemetery of the Isola Sacra (Porto, near Rome). More than three hundred small amphorae, less than ten centimeters high and crudely scratched with the name of the humble dead they enclose, have been found near the Appian Way.

From the Augustan Age onward, however, the right to a written funerary record spread even to members of the middle and lower-middle classes of society and was taken up by the freedmen in a particular way. They adopted the idea of recording a personal *res gestae*, but transformed it from the registration of a public *cursus honorum* into a resonant declaration of membership in a particular work milieu or a specific community of service. Typical from this point of view is the celebrated Roman funerary monument of the baker Marcus Vergilius Eurysaces, which has remained in situ (there is another inscription dedicated to his wife that is now in the Palazzo dei Conservatori on the Capitoline) on which the writing is arranged along a cornice brilliantly inserted between the architectural elements representing the oven and trade of the deceased.

There were other innovations generated by the funerary culture of the freedmen, in particular, the preference for single-family tombs and hence for a tombstone shared by several individuals of different generations. There was also the predilection for individual and group portraits, with a resulting increase in the illustrated spaces on the tombstone. Already in the first century B.C. this led, in some at least of the funerary inscriptions of freedmen, to a displacement of the writing spaces. Whereas there had been just one, strictly separated from the rest of the monument, they multiplied variously. The written and illustrated spaces sometimes trespassed on each other, and the extremely rigid boundary of official and "normal" epigraphy constituted by the cornice was infringed. Inevitably, in these cases, the alignment becomes erratic, the arrangement of the lines capricious (sometimes clustered into the gaps between illustrated elements), and the shape of the letters irregular. The current epigraphical norm, if not broken, was certainly dented by these new and singular graphico-spatial strategies. Two first-century B.C. funerary monuments can serve as examples: first, the altar of Lucius Avillius Dionisius, freedman "conditor" of the red faction in the circus games, in which the unframed and irregularly compressed writing fills three different spaces, running over itself around the figuration (Rome, Capitoline Museum); then, the tabernacle stele, structured on two orders, of the shipwright Publius Longidienus, with portraits of four members of the family and three epigraphic texts, variously arranged.

The writing, on the other hand, was often less terse and more diffuse than in inscriptions of higher rank and more traditional form, with a consequent need to enlarge the space for writing, thicker clustering of the letters, and compression of the lines. Especially in the provinces (particularly in Gaul and on the Rhine), funerary inscriptions for freedmen and soldiers of the first and second centuries have an expansive narrative discourse instead of the *cursus honorum*, an account of the deceased's life and even his manner of death as part of a report dense in events and living people.

5.   The very diversity of the burial modes of ancient civilization, from the imposing mausoleum to the simple plaque in a columbarium, very often led to a displacement of the writing, particularly in complex monuments. However, usually (and especially in more official cases) this occurred in obedience to the traditional graphic norm and not in its breach. Very often it is on the more simple monuments that one finds a new and freer use of funerary writing. There remains, however, the striking fact of the spread of a different graphic typology—what is known as "rustic"—in epigraphy, funerary and otherwise, during the second and third centuries. The term is not to be taken as when used of the book, but understood in the high and narrow sense proper to the mural and to brushwork on domestic pottery—something very much part of the daily life of the average Roman.

As we know, a high percentage of Roman funerary inscriptions of the imperial period are military epitaphs from the provinces. It is not difficult to see in them three characteristic features that represent, if not adaptations of the norm, then significant modifications of it:

1. The presence of the likeness, often with official characterization (arms, uniforms), which overwhelms the writing space.

2. Writing that often escapes from its allotted space to take over part of the cornice.

3. Awkward layout meant to correct the poor planning of space: the insertion of smaller letters inside larger ones, or of ligatures between neighboring letters, something frequent in provincial epigraphy in any case.

In certain examples—such as that of the Germanic funerary stele of the *miles* Marcus Braetius of the XIII Gemina Legion (9–17 A.D.), which is badly laid out in six lines—one finds the very negation of the model of the squared epigraphical capital and the rendering of certain letters in cursive, such as the *A*.

Outside the military and provincial milieu, in Italy itself, perhaps in Rome itself, the graphic language used to record the dead shows significant changes in the second and third centuries. In certain second-century funerary inscriptions from the Isola Sacra, numerous cursive or even minuscule elements appear. A well-known example of the kind is the funerary epigraph of the boys Torquatianus and Lelianus, dated from the first or second century. It is written entirely in cursive capitals, almost as if on a waxed tablet. The alignment is uncertain, the size of the letter decreases in the last two lines, and the writing space is not marked off. Though it hardly fits in with the rest of surviving epigraphy, it is probable that this extremely humble inscription, badly formulated and badly cut, is just one example of a product widespread among the lower levels of the urban population.

The impression one gets from the study of the formal aspects of inscriptions of the imperial age is that gradually but certainly, from the final phase of the first century onward, anomalous formal usages appeared for a variety of reasons alongside and in contrast with the dominant graphic norm. It would seem that in the provinces, and in socially and culturally marginal milieus of Italy and Rome itself, graphico-spatial solutions one cannot call "canonical," innovative practices and modes of constructing a written language of death, arose haphazardly out of indifference or ignorance. Nowhere and in no case, however, does it seem that these symptoms of graphic strain and formal in-

ventiveness come close to outlining or proposing an overall and organically alternative norm to the highly geometric terseness of official
and cultivated usage proposed (and imposed) by the culture of death
among the upper classes of Roman society. That was to require a profound upheaval, something more than a stretching of the formal and
graphic structures of funerary inscriptions, something that modified
the very meaning of the social relationship with death and with the
dead: a new ideology, a new religious conviction.

The Names and the Crosses

1. The Christians very soon learned to write their dead. They did it, however, within an overall perspective and using strategies of communication and expression very different from those of pagan tradition generally. The reasons for this were, first and foremost, their proclaimed egalitarian stance: "Amongst us," as Lactantius writes with pride, "there is no difference between slaves and masters" (*Divinatum institutionum libri*, 5, 14–15); then, because of the ideological indifference to the cult of dead bodies well expressed by Augustine: "there is no feeling in a dead body" (*De cura pro mortuis gerenda*, Migne, *Patrologia latina*, 40, col. 594), and again: "all these things, that is, taking care of the funeral, the condition of the burial, the pomp of the ceremony, are a greater consolation to the living than a help to the dead" (ibid.). He also had to admit, though, that burial was always a duty of humanity (ibid., col. 595) and that tombs provided an occasion to pray for the salvation of the dead (ibid., col. 596). This apart, at least in the earliest period, between the third and fourth centuries, the choice of burial in large underground hypogea entailed very different physical conditions and siting for the practice and diffusion of funerary writing than those that had characterized traditional pagan and official practices, conditions that made it difficult, if not impossible, to reproduce customary models automatically.

In the earliest paleo-Christian cemetery areas (the first is that of Saint Callixtus in Rome, dating from the papacy of Pope Zephirinus, 198–217) the presence of loculi, of niches, and of graves with several levels (*formae*) structured the presence of writing spaces in a new way. The carving of a tombstone meant dealing with variously shaped spaces, sometimes oblong and always restricted, on which a text had to be arranged that was also—at least in the earliest period—usually very limited in its formulas and that stood out as Christian not so much, or not only, by the use of determined expressions of obvious religious import as by its use of symbols—the Constantinian monogram, the fish, the palm, the dove, and so on.

Very often, the traditional technique of carving on the stone was accompanied, or rather replaced, by that of writing in minium with a brush on terracotta tiles, a poor technique that certainly did not lend itself to long and complex texts and that usually went along with inscriptions of utter simplicity, such as the "Peace be with you, Filumena" dedicated to the humble member of the faithful in Rome who for centuries was taken for a saint.

2.   The text was thus reduced to the essentials, and out of obvious ideological and demonstrative humility, so was the designation of the deceased. The use of the *tria nomina* was effectively abolished, there was drastic reduction of the *duo nomina* (10.5 percent in the cemetery of Saints Marcus and Marcellianus and Damasus), and the forename was generally adopted. This matched the vision of the catacomb as a communal cemetery area where the dead brethren were all equal before God and their fellows, all merited the same respect, and all were in expectation of the same miraculous process of reincarnation. Where life after death was stressed as more important than earthly life, the dead were considered the ones who were truly alive, the *dies natalis* was thus that of death, not birth, and the cemetery was seen as a city of those who had passed on and were periodically honored by the living. Not surprisingly, this concentration on a life beyond the grave sometimes led to the name of the deceased being left off the loculus or replaced by sequences of letters that had purely magical significance.

What has been called the "archaic laconicism" of the earliest paleo-Christian inscriptions carried with it a rejection of the traditional formulaic schema of antique funerary epigraphy, where the succession of the parts was fixed and rich, and the elegy and the *cursus honorum* constituted the very heart of the composition. The linear geometrical construction of pagan epigraphy, diffuse and hence hierarchically laid out according to fixed schemes, no longer served for the organization, display, and comprehension of a textual structure reduced to the succession of a few words centering on a forename and all easily identified.

The arrangement of the words might be free, linearity was a matter of choice, the division between space for text and space for figuration was in practice rejected, and the conception of the epigraph as a "page" architectonically constructed as a linear composition largely derived from the book was ignored.

One of the elements of greatest significance in the graphic texture of the earliest paleo-Christian epigraphy is the insertion by the stone carver of figurative symbols within and in connection with the text, sometimes to break it up and sometimes to give it visual rhythm, as it were. As I already have said, these symbols are simple and essential, in certain cases occurring alone, but often in pairs: the dove with the olive branch in its beak, the anchor, the fish, the vase of the *refrigerium*, the peacock, as well as the so-called "apocalyptic" letters (*A* and *Ω*), the *T* as cross, and the already mentioned *chrismon*, or Constantinian monogram—a superimposed *X* and *P*—often flanked by the apocalyptic letters, sometimes in reverse order.

These symbols sometimes stand as marginal comment on or conclusion to the text and are sometimes internal to it, with the result that they break the *consecutio*, split it into different and contrasting portions, and give it spatial and formal movement. The outcome is a new and extremely lively complex of signs, no longer arranged in a linear schema, one line above the next, but centering on groups of letters and signs linked in a variety of ways and laid out in deliberately chaotic fashion within a space no longer firmly bounded by a cornice, as in the traditional formal model, but left free, and hence freely occupied.

Given the abundance and geographic spread of the examples, it is difficult to chart the variety of ways in which the different elements are placed. The phenomenon was certainly widespread and uniform throughout the western provinces, considerably less so, as we will see, in Africa. In certain cases, the alphabetical symbols constitute the decisive element in the layout of the writing space and—as in the disquieting inscription to Agapis from the Roman cemetery of Ottavilla— confine the name to a marginal position or sharply divide the text. The epitaph of the girl child Victorina, for example, is split into two columns by a *chrismon* with apocalyptic letters. In numerous other cases, it is the iconographic elements that displace and demote the text to a clearly subordinate position. The text, for example, of a fragment from the Roman cemetery of saints Peter and Marcellinus, dating from 307, is broken and set to one side, while two epitaphs from the same workshop give prominence to the image of a peacock upsetting a basket of flowers, with the vase of the *refrigerium* alongside. It is also the case in the epitaph of Pontaza, where the text appears as a marginal insertion in a rich and lively figurative context.

In various cases, the iconographic element consists of a standing human figure, representing the dead in the pose of a suppliant or an offerer. In these cases, also, the clear dominance of the image relegates the text to a marginal position or breaks the arrangement by splitting it into several segments. This is the case with the epitaph of Titus Eupor, from the Roman cemetery of Pretestato, where the inscription straggles over three columns. It also occurs in the truly unusual cases of "Florentia dulcissima," where the text is arranged vertically on an altar, with the figure of an offerer standing by, and in that of Secundilla, where it is inscribed, again vertically, on a column supporting the bust of a suppliant, in front of which stands a dove.

In many of these aspects, paleo-Christian epigraphy reflects or copies models from contemporary Roman provincial and military epigraphy, though the latter hardly ever reaches such a degree of graphic disarray and such insistence on an assortment of figural and verbal elements. What strikes one as the real novelty here is the intrusion into the writing space of an iconographic element made up of densely packed and highly meaningful religious symbols. They helped constitute a wholly religious and self-referential funerary epigraphy, the purpose of which was to give voice to the chorus of the living and the dead, of the witnesses (the martyrs) and the *fratres*, of God and man.

3.   Among the dead of the Christian funerary cult, the martyrs stood out as a particular and privileged point of reference. They were the dead par excellence, sanctified by their sacrifice, a privileged category of intermediaries between the living and God, "advocates" for the faithful in the beyond. To be a dead martyr meant, of course, to have a burial place, and the burial places of martyrs were the object of a particular cult. Often lodged or englobed within churches, they were the focus of religious ceremonies at which crowds of the faithful, the active element in the cult, came together. This cult is one of the more striking aspects of the general paleo-Christian funerary culture and shaped many particular activities, among which writing stands out.

Indeed, the martyrs were not only the dead par excellence, they are also the most "written" members of the Christian sepulchral universe. From the second half of the third century onward, it became increasingly the custom for visitors to the catacombs and the burial places of martyrs to write their own and others' names, along with devout invocations, as close as possible to the saintly body. The names were almost always scratched on the wall by the visitors themselves, though on occasion one can deduce the mediation of "surrogate writers," custodians of the cemetery or clerics.

The graffiti inscribed sometime between 290 and 315 A.D. on wall "g" underground at Saint Peter's in Rome are an eloquent example of the frenetic superimposition of different writings in the same tiny space, without concern for what was already written or any eye to graphic ordering and legibility. The message, beseeching the martyr's intercession for the writer's soul, or very often for those of the dear departed, was not, of course, addressed to the living, but solely to the chosen intermediary, who could have no difficulty in receiving it, even if overwritten by others and illegible to human eyes. Naturally, it was important that the message be set down as close as possible to the saint's body, not merely that it might reach him in safety, but so that the name—that particular name written in that particular place— might share in the aura of salvation emanated by the sacred body.

The graffiti of visitors to what is known as the *triclia* of San Sebastiano on the Appian Way, dating from the last four decades of the third century and inscribed by more than two hundred unskilled hands in large, crude, and unsteady capitals, sometimes embellished with pretentious ornamental elements, is another Roman example of people writing their "own" dead. Many examples are in the Greek alphabet and language, others are written in Latin with Greek characters. Individual writers commend themselves or their relatives to Peter and Paul, sometimes long lists of names are preceded by expressions such as "pray for," "entreat for," or "keep in mind." At least in one case, the writer includes other visitors in his plea: "Paul and Peter, and you, the reader, keep in mind." Generally, however, the message is addressed directly and exclusively to the holy martyrs, to whom the writer commends himself in stereotyped formulas, sometimes suggested, perhaps, by the resident clerics or patterned on the earlier writings.

The use of writing "one's" dead, establishing a direct dialogue with them and binding to them the name of the person commended in magical fashion by inscribing the corresponding letters as close as possible to the body of the dead intermediary, was very widespread. It was permitted, if not controlled and regulated (within the limits of the possible), by those in charge of the various cemeteries and places of burial, who may sometimes have had a direct hand in it.

The credence that being near, contiguous, to the body of a saint would promote the health of the soul was widespread in paleo-Christian funerary culture. Seen from this standpoint, the passage from writing to burial, that is, from the name to the body, was natural. Indeed, if it profited the souls of the dead that their names be set next to the tomb of a martyr, more still might be gained by laying their bodies close to a martyr's tomb. This resulted in the well-known phenomenon of "privileged" burials, with all the disturbances and abuses connected with it. It was a practice widely engaged in and exploited both by the *fossores*, the gravediggers who traded in tomb spaces, and, probably for reasons of prestige, even by the middling clergy (priests) responsible for individual cemeteries.

The fact was, indeed, had to be, or ended by being, stressed in explicit declarations of physical closeness and sometimes even of the stratification of the burial in such phrases as: "close to the remains"; "above the bones of the saintly body"; "next to the burial pit of the Lord"; "next to the saintly body"; and "between the martyrs." Hence, we find in Christian cemeteries areas in which the concentration not only of bodies, but of writing is very high and follows—in its spatial arrangement, layout, and sometimes in its overlayering—criteria and purposes far removed, not least for this reason, from the criteria and the purposes behind the ordered and hierarchic arrangement of pagan funerary epigraphy.

The debatable ideology of "privileged" burial places stirred reaction and polemic. In *De cura pro mortuis gerenda*, the small treatise already mentioned, Augustine explicitly replies to Paulinus's query—whether it can benefit anyone after death that his body be buried close to the tomb of a saint—that deserts are gained in life, not after death, and that the mode of burial cannot alter judgment on behavior in life. The epitaph of Sabinus, a Roman archdeacon, now in San Lorenzo (*Inscriptiones christianae Urbis Romae septimo saeculo antiquiores*, no. 18017) states: "To build in body . . . tombs for the pious is not a good work; it does not help, but rather hurts: instead, let us reach out to them in soul." The phenomenon continued to spread despite the polemics. The burial places of the most important and influential members of the community, laity or clergy as might be, were set apart from those of the ordinary faithful, who had neither the standing nor the means to get themselves a burial place that was both a mark of distinction and, for the purposes of life after death, in some way a comfort also.

Writing, used often in new and more freely expressive forms and more functionally employed than in the past, was instrument and evidence in the whole process. Presence and absence, the crowding together and the setting apart of bodies and writing, never occurred by chance. They obeyed precise rules dictated, according to the occasion, by the imagined hierarchy of the dead, by the religious ideology and purposes of living individuals, and by the social prestige of the family nuclei involved.

4.   After Rome, where there is a concentration of about forty-five thousand paleo-Christian inscriptions, the next largest quantity of Christian funerary writing comes from pre-Arab Africa, especially from the Africa of the fifth and sixth centuries, with all its variety of political, administrative, cultural, and ethnic arrangements.

Christian Africa does not seem to have borrowed the terms of its funerary production from Rome; indeed, it seems to have disregarded its trends and novelties. Its own epigraphic production, rich, various, and above all highly original, reached its peak during the sixth century, that is, in the age of Justinian, on the very eve of the final collapse of classical and Christian religious and cultural tradition brought about by the Arab invasion.

When one looks at African Christian epigraphs, often characterized by a dense fabric of carefully aligned text, one becomes aware of the extent to which the writing of death on the southern shore of the Mediterranean developed according to stylistic patterns very different from those current in the Roman catacombs. This does not mean that in Africa, and in late paleo-Christian Africa, between Vandals and Byzantines, there were no manifestations of novelty and originality in the graphic field. Where they did exist, however, they served to characterize a writing system that kept largely to the old rules of linearity and homogeneity in letter size.

Though many differences exist from center to center and area to area of Christian Africa, certain elements and features can be considered common or at least very widespread.

These characteristics may be listed as follows: an almost generalized regularity of alignment, often supported by visible ruling, sometimes emphatically doubled; a limited presence, or strict marginalization, of figural and ornamental motifs, used, when they exist, to frame, delimit, or surround the text, never to divide it or disturb the linear order; a widespread use of mosaic in epitaphs, with the presence, in this case clear and evident, of iconographic elements and a consequent tighter adherence to traditional graphic forms; the innovative placing of the texts on *mensae* and pavements (if mosaic); the relative richness and complexity of the texts, which are often prolix; and especially, from a strictly graphic standpoint, the presence of particular alphabetic forms, such as the capital *L* with foot slanting sharply downward, the frequent presence of the backward *S*, the occurrence of Greek or grecizing elements (especially in the Byzantine period), such as the *B* with detached loops, the *D* in delta form, and the *K* used instead of the *C*; and finally the insertion of minuscule letters (for example *q*) in a context of capitals, and the writing of entire epitaphs in minuscule, a form in any case of local origin.

What seems to have most obviously characterized the funerary epigraphy of paleo-Christian Africa is a veritable religion of funerary writing, used widely and with emphatic solemnity both on individual epitaphs and overall within the ambit of the various cemetery areas, often achieving remarkable levels of originality of expression. Fevrier was not wrong when he remarked on the monumentality of the late epitaphs and said that it tended to "preserve the dignity of the writing of funerary inscriptions."

The phenomenon is particularly evident in the *memoria martyrum* of the basilica of Candidus in Haïdra (Tunisia). This is a proper cenotaph, set up in the Byzantine period to record 34 martyrs killed during the persecution of Diocletian, on which writing looms large in the form of a long and twice-repeated inscription, first on a *tabula ansata* thickly covered in seven long lines of text and again vertically on the mosaic covering the resting place of the bodies. Two further epitaphs of noteworthy figures from the same locality, Bishop Melleus (578–79) and the *defensor civitatis* Mustelus, have strictly traditional layout, given visual rhythm and reinforcement by various *signa crucis*, the sole symbolic elements present.

Indeed, rather than having such elements, funerary writing throughout Christian Africa has accentuated ornamental graphisms, such as the forking of the uprights, cuts reinforcing and complementing the feet and heads of certain letters (the *A*, for example), ruled lines, and deep carving. There was a taste in exhibited writing that graphic exaggeration, influenced directly by the neighboring Greek models, tended to make more visible, more evident, and more communicative, especially in epitaphs dedicated to the ecclesiastical hierarchy and in more solemn inscriptions. A taste that, even if in different ways, lasted into the very late funerary inscriptions of Ain-Zara (not dated) and of En-Ngila (tenth century), in the very middle of the early Middle Ages, which are rich in ornamental flourishes and embellishment of line that betray direct Coptic and even Arabic stylistic influences.

5.   In Italy, and in particular in Rome, a graphic reaction of a neo-classical and conservative bent had already begun in the second half of the fourth century, with the return or recovery, even if artificial and manipulatory, of the traditional graphic norms; the composition of long verse epitaphs produced by and for higher circles of the ecclesiastical hierarchy; and an emphasis on epigraphic models characterized by full linearity, homogeneity of letter size, and the elimination of figured elements.

Between 365 and 384, the principal promoter of this remarkable phenomenon was Pope Damasus, a refined man of letters, stubborn sustainer of the primacy of Rome, creator of basilicas, and restorer of the cult of the martyrs. To him are owed numerous short odes dedicated to the tombs of the martyrs in the Roman catacombs he restored, odes that a graphic artist of great ability, Philocalus, designed for carving on marble slabs in monumental capitals of great geometric strictness and high formal expressivity based on a sharp contrast of thick and thin and on the ornamental effect of eye-catching curlicues added to the verticals.

Damasus and Philocalus engaged in a veritable "program of graphic exhibition" centering on the most highly symbolic sites of Christian worship in Rome and on its funerary tradition. The project had a lasting influence on later local epigraphic tradition, both because of the strategic placing of their efforts and because of their sharp stylistic characterization.

Damasus's initiative also represented an important moment in the process of "churchifying" the cult of the martyrs that occurred in Rome between the fourth and sixth centuries and that led to the transformation of the catacombs into a series of chapels and later to the translation of relics to basilicas and churches in the city and outside. All that Rome did in this was to anticipate a more general phenomenon. As we know, imperial legislation prohibited burial within the city walls, and in 381–82, Valentinian, Gratian, and Theodosius again decreed that all the remains of the dead should be buried outside the City, enclosed in urns or sarcophagi. But in time, the ban was neglected everywhere, especially for members of the upper hierarchy, the only people who still enjoyed the privilege of having written epitaphs on their tombs.

As Sidonius Apollinaris was traveling between Lyons and Clermont in 469, he spotted some thieves trying to break into his grandfather's tomb. He stopped them, and finding that the tomb lacked any identifying marker, he decided to compose a long verse inscription. He went on to get it inscribed, despite the doubts he expressed in a letter to his son: "but see the stone carver makes no mistake in it, because, whatever the cause, the ill-intentioned reader will lay the responsibility more at my door than his."

The long verse epitaphs reserved for the illustrious were small literary works and usually were executed with all the requisite graphic care. The fact that they were set up within the city walls and in churches merely increased their solemnity and symbolic value. It was no accident that bishops, who from the last quarter of the fourth century onward were already being buried in privileged positions, began to be interred in the urban churches, beginning in the middle of the fifth century.

Around the end of the fourth century and the beginning of the fifth, a funerary epigraphy of high formal quality began to develop in Rome, a new interpretation of the Philocalus model. It modified the strict canon and extended the ornamental curlicue motif to the horizontal strokes of letters, as can be seen in the 471 epitaph of the priest Felix and that of Petronia (d. 472), wife of Felix the Deacon (later Pope Felix III), son of the former. During the sixth century, the monumentalization of funerary epigraphy dedicated to illustrious figures in the city's hierarchy became more emphatic, especially during the Byzantine period. Evidence for this includes the 555 epitaph of the priest

Marea in Santa Maria in Trastevere; the very elegant one, with double ruling, of an unknown bishop who died in 569, now in the basilica of Sant' Alessandro on the Via Nomentana; and the very curious one of the notary Eugenius, dating from 578, where the text is split between a centrally placed portion and two lateral tondi.

The epigraphic model visible in the fragments of the tomb inscription of Gregory the Great (d. 604) is of great and ancient dignity, characterized by imposingly wide letters and a calligraphic elegance of line. It confirms the existence in Rome of an unbroken formal tradition of "high" funerary epigraphy that had lasted over several centuries and that was characterized by singular rehandling of the classical graphic model. At the dawn of the seventh century, during the short-lived triumph of a form of funerary writing aimed at celebrating the last splendors of a select "Roman" ecclesiastical aristocracy, the traumatic renewal brought about in graphic usage by the revolution of the catacombs was finally forgotten and the underground cities of the dead became almost completely neglected.

Writing the Great

1.   The early Middle Ages in Europe (especially in the west) was a period in which almost all the dead remained once again unwritten. In practice, the so-called "Dark Ages" abandoned exhibited writing and its variegated uses. Funerary language very largely went back to images, symbols, and configurations, abandoning the written word. The peoples of the north, the German founders of the new kingdoms, customarily buried their dead in cemeteries open to the skies, where individual tombs were marked by signs and images. The catacombs, veritable underground cities of writing, were giving way to the ancient European burial place without writing.

This narrowing in the use of exhibited writing was certainly due to the more general reduction of written culture as a whole, to the collapse of the ancient school system, to growing illiteracy, and to the decline of the city and of public administration. It was also, however, a matter of the affirmation of a culture—in our case, funerary—that had remote roots, one that adopted expressive codes at variance with those of classical Mediterranean civilization and that preferred "transmission through iconic signs and visual reception" to that based on written communication. In such a situation, funerary writing, even when employed, could have only the residual, purely iconic value held during the same period by coins. Marking out the dead became prevalently and inevitably symbolic and iconographic once again, often more internal (a function, that is, of lavish grave goods) than external.

Despite this, the practice of exhibited funerary writing survived through the seventh and eighth centuries, though production was very much smaller. It was monopolized by the urban high clergy and was used on the one hand for the celebration of the ecclesiastical hierarchy and of the saintly protectors of churches and the city, and on the other by local lay elites, from sovereigns and rulers of lands to benefactors of churches and monasteries. This graphic exhibition, concentrated in churches, occurred in parallel with the transfer of the burial places of bishops and high-ranking clergy to churches outside cities—but to urban ones also, at least from the second half of the sixth century onward, and more intensely, beginning in the seventh century. The "churchifying" of funerary writing and its exclusive use by the ruling elites were in fact parallel phenomena. Evidence for this is provided by various legal measures. A capitulary of 813, for example, limited burial in churches to those who belonged to certain precise categories—bishops, abbots, and priests "faithful and good"—while Theodulf of Orléans excluded priests and righteous men of particular merit from the general ban and so marked out the confines of a true aristocracy of churchmen and "particular" members of the laity.

As for the numerical decrease in epigraphs, inspection of the first thirteen volumes of the *Corpus des inscriptions de la France médiévale* reveals that of the 357 epitaphs extant and reproduced, only 10 come from the period between the seventh and tenth centuries, and of these, a minimal part can be dated to the seventh and eighth centuries. The last great period of exhibited funerary writing in western Europe was, in fact, the sixth century. It enabled the survival for some decades everywhere, but more in Italy than anywhere else, of the ancient world's system of written culture. A considerable production of funerary inscriptions continued for almost the whole century, in both Italy and Gaul, by then under the Franks. In a passage of his *Liber in gloria confessorum*, Gregory of Tours, an eyewitness to the tumultuous events under the first Merovingian monarchy, tells of a chapel rich in tombs "in which there are many tombs sculpted in Parian marble, in which holy men and religious women repose; there are also many tombs of believers." And he goes on to add that on one of them "there is the inscription: to the sacred memory of Galla." And Venantius Fortunatus, an Italian poet active in Merovingian Gaul, has left a conspicuous number of verse epitaphs in honor of bishops, churchmen, and women, at least some of which must have been intended for inscription on marble and for public exhibition.

Some of the Italian verse epitaphs from that century are remarkable examples of funerary epigraphy laid out according to the ancient dictates: that of the great poet Ennodius (d. 521) in the basilica of San

Michele in his native Pavia, classical in its solemn impagination; and the large epitaph of Bishop Agrippinus of the Isola Comacina, now in the church of Sant' Eufemia d'Isola (Como), which displays great mastery of impagination and layout, even if the graphic style is "modern." The survival, in Italy especially, of a number of exhibited epigraphical products from the late antique period undoubtedly provided later centuries with a wealth of graphic styles to which the early medieval practitioners periodically turned for authoritative models, inspiration, and sometimes even to borrow their formal aspects.

2.   This was not the case always or everywhere. There were regions where the ancient models did not exist or were incapable of exerting any real influence. The result was a free and unsystematic quest for new spatial and graphic solutions in which abstract figural elements often go along with writing. It was a widespread and chaotic phenomenon, more common in the smaller centers than in large ones with ancient traditions, and present more in the area of the Merovingian kingdom than in Lombard Italy, but significant examples of it are to be found everywhere. Dating from as early as 585, the tombstone of Boetius, bishop of Carpentras, has a small area in the upper section with four lines of writing, while the remaining space is occupied by a large cross flanked by round and square ornamental motifs. The epitaph of Trasemirus, from Mandourel (Aube), dating from about 600, consists of a sidelong slab, the entire central area of which is occupied by three stylized crosses and two facing doves, while the inscription, for which no proper space was provided, is relegated to just two of the four sectors of the cornice. In the extremely rational solution—absolutely innovative, since no earlier example is known—adopted in Jouarre for the cenotaph of the first abbess of the local monastery, Saint Theodechildes, the writing is arranged in several parallel strips, separated by bands of ornamental roundels. The epitaph of Bertesindis and Raudoald, from Mainz, is very much influenced by paleo-Christian precedents, and the writing space is cramped between two figured areas, one occupied by crosses, the other by three segments of purely ornamental decoration, creating a highly evocative effect.

From the Rhineland come numerous examples of a graphic style that can be considered the Franco-Germanic epigraphical model of the sixth and seventh centuries. They are characterized by the use of a triangular *D*, minuscule *q* above the line, *L* with a downward sloping baseline, a *G* consisting of two opposing curves, the use of ornamental forks at the end of the uprights and of letters of smaller size (especially the *o*) often placed inside others. But sometimes the absence of any norm of layout, a total unconcern with legibility, and a propensity for extreme liberties in letter shapes leads to a crowding of signs that allows for no more than a purely visual reading. This is the case with the epitaph of Bernard in the Musée des Augustins in Toulouse, dating from the eighth century, in which the eight lines of text, of letters varying in size, consist of an inextricable and highly evocative tangle of ligatures, overlappings, and use of letters different one from the next.

The tombstone of the priest Gaudiris of Savigliano is remarkable for northern Italy. The field is occupied by a large cross on which the text of the epitaph proper is inscribed horizontally and vertically, while further writing is inserted in the two upper squares of the field, including on the left the signature of the creator of the work, "Germanius," who describes himself as "master of marble work."

3.   The symbolic element of the cross also appears in three well-known Milanese funerary epigraphs dating from the seventh century, those of Aldus, Manfred, and Odelbert. These provide the first evidence of a graphic style featuring the slenderness of line and the elongation and narrowing of the letter shapes that was to become proper to the great Lombard epigraphy of the eighth century. But in these first examples, the figurative element is strongly marked and divides or hems in the epigraphical text, even though set out in full. The general arrangement thus recalls both the paleo-Christian tradition and notions derived from the book, like the motif of the large cross occupying the whole field in the epitaphs of Aldus and Manfred, reminiscent of rich silver bindings, or like the arch that frames the epitaph of Odelbert, typical of late antique illumination.

It is difficult to specify what the designers of the official eighth-century Pavia epitaphs took as models. It is clear, however, that the epitaphs display a conscious use of a solemn funerary style, a new epigraphical script, and spatial arrangements that go back to late antique tradition, though employed in an entirely original way.

Pavia was the capital of the Lombards, and the epitaphs that best represent the stylistic novelty and diversity of solutions possible within a program of graphic celebration of illustrious figures are dedicated to members of the ruling dynasty.

The major innovations in the epigraphic style that may properly be described as "Pavian," even if not exclusive to the capital of the kingdom, are the relationship between ornamental motifs from the late antique tradition, used as framing devices or to divide the internal space into strips, and the writing, which once again entirely—or all but—occupies the field in firm and securely linear progression; the alternation of vertical and horizontal arrangement of text, with layout in one or two columns, respectively; the graphic style, consisting of long, slender capitals with filiform cuts, enriched by ornamental elements and by particular "Greek" forms (the *A*, the *M*, the *N*), and by a *Q* with the tail taken up inside, a late antique motif widespread in the Merovingian area of influence. It is possible that this stylization arose in the same milieu of cultivated Pavian churchmen that created the long verse texts of the epitaphs and that there was a translation into stone of graphic suggestions drawn from the decorative apparatus of contemporary luxury liturgical codices.

The epitaph of Queen Ragintruda (around 740–50), with its vertical layout, its alternation of packed lines and half-empty lines, with ivy leaves and stylized fruits acting as punctuation, is a striking example of graphico-aesthetic balance, as are, in their different ways, the analogous epitaph of Cunicperga, the abbess daughter of King Cunipert, arranged horizontally in two columns, its stern and dignified layout set off by ligatures between adjacent letters, and the tombstone of Audoaldus, duke of Liguria, dating from 763, in which the vertical single-column layout is imaginatively parsed by an ornamental strip dividing the text in two and separating a dense upper portion of seven lines from a lower section spread over twelve lines of differing length, concluded in its turn by a second strip of ornament. In the view of Nicolete Gray the latter is "the most beautiful" of Pavian tombstones.

But this graphic stylization was not restricted to Pavia. Other examples are the epitaph of Bishop Cumianus, now in Bobbio, to which Pietro Toesca already has drawn attention, signed by a "Iohannes magister" and dating from 736, with its double frame of ornamental motifs and thick graphic embroidery of thin, narrow capitals; and the 773 epitaph of Bishop Vitalianus of Osimo, laid out in ten lines set off by a large, ornamented frame. In these (and in other analogous cases) one is dealing with artifacts meant to celebrate the highest levels of the Lombard ecclesiastical hierarchy, its history, and its splendors, an enterprise administered by cultivated members of the clergy who were drawing on the models that had served to consecrate the memory of the national dynasty. If there is one place where "written death" had a precise political and cultural message, it was the Lombard kingdom in the eighth century between Liutprand and Desiderius, a moment at which a reawakening of tradition and experimental innovation, ecclesiastical hierarchy and royalty, miraculously conspired together.

4.   On Christmas Day 795, the great Pope Hadrian I died in Rome. He was Roman in culture and descent, foe to the Lombards and friend to the Franks, and linked by firm bonds of political alliance to Charlemagne. Since the pope had earned the gratitude of the Franks, it was by the express will of Charlemagne that his funerary epitaph was not composed and fashioned in Rome, but in France, the first and last occasion of the kind. Presumably, some months or even a year later, the epitaph arrived from France to be set up in Saint Peter's, and in the portico of the new Saint Peter's it can still be seen today.

This epitaph, inscribed on black marble with a verse text that is perhaps the work of Alcuin, was a very important epigraphic novelty in the Rome of the time. Splendidly laid out in forty lines (it consists of twenty elegiac couplets) framed by a strip with spiral plant motifs, the geometrically balanced form of the letters, the skillful filling of the writing space, and the triangular cut immediately create the impression of a return to the antique. But the ligatures between adjacent letters, the raising of the *T*, and the ornamental elements present in certain letters suggest an inspiration based less on direct imitation of official tombstones of the classical period than on such late antique luxury codices in monumental capitals as the Codex Augusteus, the Codex Sangallensis, or even the *tituli* of other sixth-century codices, such as the *Agrimensores* of Wolfenbüttel.

In short, in order to celebrate the dead, or better, the most illustrious of them, they turned back to the past, to the great graphic and spatial models of the late antique period, to the Damasine and post-Damasine tradition. As we know, the Carolingian renaissance in writing brought back graphic styles that had been neglected for centuries or that had diverged profoundly from the original models: the monumental capital, the rustic capital, the uncial, the half uncial, even the so-called "quarter uncial." The phenomenon involved not just the book, but epigraphy as well, as shown by the epitaph of Hadrian I, though it, too, was based on book models. It spread from the nerve center of the Carolingian court to the lands belonging (after Christmas 800) to the newly founded Holy Roman Empire, or at least to certain important centers within it.

Writing the dead "in ancient fashion" did not in fact spread uniformly throughout Carolingian Europe, and one may doubt that it was taken up in Rome itself, where the epitaph of Hadrian I does not seem to have been a directly imitated model, but rather a fount of encouragement for the old classicizing and traditionalist bent that already existed there. This would explain, for example, the regular, square capitals of the epitaph of Paul the Levite in the portico of San Lorenzo in Lucina, which should probably be dated to somewhere in the first half of the ninth century, rather than to 783, as it has been. It also explains the splendid epitaph of Pope Nicholas I (d. 867), an imposing example of the monumental capital, with strong cut and square forms, barely lightened by ornamental curlicues deriving from the tradition of Rome. Finally (but we are in 893, almost at the end of the ninth century), it explains the epitaph of the *superista* Demetrius—"the most beautiful inscription" of the period according to Gray—an example of the continuity in the great classicizing epigraphy reserved in Rome for the illustrious dead.

Lombard Benevento, enclosed within the graphic culture known for this reason as Beneventan and untouched by the graphic renaissance beyond the Alps, stood in proud and solitary isolation from this tradition and the Carolingian models. Like the kings of Pavia, the princes of Benevento, who after the collapse of the kingdom in 774 had kept up the traditions of their race in Lombardy Minor, put their tombstones in the main church of their capital, in this case Santa Sofia di Benevento. Like the kings of Pavia, they, too, employed long and structured verse epitaphs and a rich, complex, and fanciful graphic style that—at least throughout the ninth century—remained generally similar in its forms to that of Pavia, though with some originality of its own. Capitals with double strokes, derived directly from the *tituli* of the contemporary southern codices, for example, appear in the epitaph of Chisa, grandchild of Sico. A long minuscule *q* is used as a majuscule, and there are ornamental signs to indicate the end of lines, perhaps the result of Roman influence. The variety of graphic solutions reached its peak in the epitaph of prince Radelgarius (d. 854), which has a grandeur in its monumental letter shapes, some of which are original, that reveals strong politico-dynastic ambition in the Benevento dynasty's "program of graphic exhibition." It is no coincidence that as many as four of the Beneventan funerary odes are the work of a single author, presumably a poet in the service of the local dynasty.

5.   Even in the extreme north of Europe, it was customary to record the illustrious dead in writing, but in ways and places completely different from those of central and southern Europe. Swedish runic inscriptions from the ninth through eleventh centuries show the affirmation of an entirely original funerary language characterized less by the use of an alphabet wholly different from that of Latin (or Greek) than by the erection of inscribed stones in the open and a strip layout highly ornamental in itself.

The earliest of these inscriptions (ninth century) comes from Rök and was dedicated by Varin to the memory of his father Vaemod. It consists of an irregularly shaped slab set upright in the ground. The face is entirely covered with writing, arranged in eight vertical lines, with two horizontal lines at the bottom. The largely vertical arrangement of the text recalls the analogous layout of the earliest Mediterranean funerary inscriptions. Later, well on into the Viking period and in the eleventh century, the layout of the writing was different, arranged strip fashion, sometimes winding snakelike in a vertical spiral or weaving in and out. It cannot have been easy in either case for the passerby, who is sometimes so invited, to read them, not least because the writing blends into the ornamental zoomorphic, plant, and cruciform motifs scattered over the field.

Sweden, the island of Gotland in particular, is extremely rich in this type of inscription. The style is firmly unitary, while the constructions are often variegated. Apart from slabs, more or less rich in ornamental elements, there are also obelisks, tall, vertically inscribed monoliths like that erected at Nävelsjö in memory of Gumar, buried at Bath, in England. Two similar large, upright granite monuments were erected at Jelling in Jutland, one by King Gorm the Old in 940 and the other in 980 by King Harald, in memory of Gorm, with a runic inscription and various ornamentations. There are further examples in England, also.

Thus, in northern Europe between the ninth and the eleventh centuries, the Germanic peoples employed their runic script in a quite original way. They created a funerary graphic language wholly independent of the late antique or paleo-Christian traditions and based on a free progression of the writing in highly decorative strips, while the open setting in a natural landscape was strongly evocative. Before it disappeared, this language probably exerted some influence on the great changes then preparing in the graphic culture of death throughout central Europe.

The Books and the Stones

⁓

1.   The European Middle Ages did not commemorate its illustrious
dead only in cemeteries and in churches, by means of the epitaphs and
inscriptions that inscribed and accompanied their remains. The European Middle Ages, and in particular the Church of the time, possessed
a written culture based on the book and on book-writing practices that
had become a corollary and indispensable aid in all religious rituals,
from the most everyday to the most solemn. In the medieval world, in
fact, almost no religious event took place without the aid of written
books, those books that we generically describe as liturgical and that
constituted the fixed structure and stay for any situation in everyday
religious life.

The ideology of the written book was profoundly internalized by
the medieval European religious community, though more perhaps in
the north than in the Mediterranean, particularly Italy, which was
more directly linked to the late antique tradition. The book represented the rule and held the record of what had taken place and what
should be done. Without writing, there was no memory.

The conception of writing as a necessary prop to memory, fundamental—at least after a certain point—in the realm of documentation,
naturally involved from a very early moment the cult of the martyrs
and the dead that every organized ecclesiastical community tended to
nurture in and for itself. But with the passage of time, the throng of
the dead whose names were to be recited during religious ceremonies
became ever larger, and the memory of the living no longer sufficed to
contain it. Already in the fifth century, there is mention of written lists
being employed by religious institutions to record the names of the
dead and the prayers due to them. The lists were generally set down

on diptychs or polytychs of ivory or bone and contained the names of the bishops of the diocese, those of governors and authorities, of the more powerful members of the clergy, and of benefactors: both the names of the dead, therefore, and those of the living who were to be publicly remembered. The Barberini diptych, a sixth-century polyptych of four (originally five) tables of ivory, now in the Louvre, is a well-known example. During the seventh century, and probably in Trier, the names of as many as three hundred and fifty members of the faithful, including a list of the kings of Austrasia, were set down in ink in six flanking columns. But written memory within religious institutions also found other lodgings, ones that enabled public reading during ceremonies. The names of the many to be commemorated were scratched on apse walls of the basilica of Parenzo, for example, between the sixth and ninth centuries. Altars also were used, and names to be remembered and recited were engraved on their surfaces at different times and often in great disarray. The most recent example to come to light is the altar of the church of Saints Peter and Paul in Reichenau-Niederzell, on which, between the tenth and eleventh centuries, the names of several hundred clergy and laity were scratched, engraved, and even written in ink, in a pure and elegant Carolingian book minuscule or in handsome "rustic" capitals.

2.   In time, progressive regulation of the liturgy and the excessive number of names to record and commemorate prompted solutions at once more complex and more practical than the simple list linked to the place where celebration took place. Names were in danger of disappearing or being canceled, and often it must have been difficult to find individual references, which might indeed get lost. It thus became necessary first to identify, then to order and compress the immense patrimony of commemorative memory that every religious community had accumulated over the centuries and recorded in a great variety of ways. Gradually and progressively, beginning in the ninth century, but particularly from the tenth century onward, this was done by splitting the various lists and creating different series of names for the living and the dead, for martyrs, bishops, and so on. Order was ensured by adopting the book as container for the individual records, since it offered ample writing space, almost infinite ease of handling, the possibility of untroubled addition, and could be easily and securely preserved.

Furthermore, the commemorative record, in contrast to that of the cemetery, was not inseparably linked to the remains, and there was no reason why it should be bound to a fixed place, in particular that of celebration. It could be put in a mobile container that could be preserved, moved, and replaced at will. The book was seen as by far the best solution for these reasons, also.

Thus, the necrology and the obituary came into being, and the recording of the dead to be commemorated became one of the many genres of book writing. The written record of certain categories of the dead was thus removed from the sphere of the stone carver and became part of the skills and practices of the amanuensis, moving out of the stone yard and the cemetery to the scriptorium and the library.

What did the celebratory record have to make clear? One piece of information was of particular importance: the date of the celebration itself, which was, for the dead, the day of their death. But the day only, not the year, which indeed is hardly ever given. The outcome was an ordering of the entries that is undoubtedly chronological in its way, but limited to a single year, the liturgical years from January 1 to December 31, marked by the succession of months, weeks, days, but never years. Hence, entries belonging to different periods and centuries can overlap in the space allotted to the single day, while those set down, perhaps by the same hand, within the span of the same year are scattered over the entire writing space available.

The necrologies, in fact, take the form of liturgical calendars, in which the deaths of the people to be commemorated are recorded next to the date. They usually consist of the abbreviation o[bitus], the deceased's name in the genitive, and some specification indicating his relationship with the commemorating community, his social position, and the reason for his inclusion in the list. Sometimes the list is laid out in several columns, distinguished by quality of person; sometimes it is simply horizontal.

Strictly speaking, there was a marked difference between a necrology, consisting of a list of names of the dead to be recited during the choir lessons, and an obituary, again a list of written names, but not for public reading. It served, instead, to recall the anniversaries founded through legacies and alms by individuals. But in practice, one comes across forms of mixed registration, such as the *Libri memoriales*, in which the dead and the living appear together.

Necrologies and obituaries were by their very nature open texts in which, while there was space available, further names were lodged. Thus, the written memory of the dead simply grew until the earliest deaths were erased to make available pages overcharged with writing, or the old lists were replaced by new books in which the contents were reordered and possibly thinned out. Memorial books of the dead were exactly like cemeteries in this. As in the cemeteries, the dead were given ordered lodging, even if only by name, and then, as space gradually ran out, the entries became more untidy, overrunning the margins, overlapping, until sections were made available again for writing by eliminating the entries that filled them or a new container for registration and funerary memory was chosen.

Seen through modern eyes, these books look like places of perpetual writing and rewriting, anticipating or—later—repeating a feature of many of the annals and chronicles from the eleventh through the thirteenth centuries, where the writer expands his work into an endless fabric of recordings, continually adding and correcting to fill out the historical report and bring it ever closer to his initial purpose. Like funerary inscriptions, necrologies and obituaries, though mainly practical and moral in character, were also to some extent works of history. Bishops and abbots, emperors, kings, and noble benefactors appear in them, along with the religious of acknowledged sanctity and lay people particularly close to the religious community. In short, they give a picture of a shared life and of the people who led and animated it over time. Even though a fixed temporal dimension is lacking, it is still there in the background, implied and immanent in the continual overlapping of names, from an eighth-century abbot to a twelfth-century count, from an eleventh-century bishop to a fourteenth-century friar.

3.   The *Liber memorialis* of the Benedictine convent of Remiremont, on the Moselle in Lorraine, is one of the earliest examples of mixed record. Begun in about 850, it was mainly written during the ninth century, with additions in the tenth, eleventh, and even twelfth centuries. The writing hands number 58 in all (many of them nuns), and there are great differences between them. However, what is most striking about this large codex, now in the Biblioteca Angelica, Rome (ms no. 10), is the jumbled arrangement of individual entries. They do not seem to follow any plan, but simply follow one another, very often beside or on top of the next, in an entirely chance, sometimes chaotic

way. This is clearly due not only to the absence of a preordained plan, but also to the long use of the book—on just 71 leaves it manages to carry 11,500 names of the living and dead—and to the participation of altogether unskilled, semiliterate writers who set down the entries with no respect for alignment at all. Clearly, what counted most in the convent of Remiremont was not the order of the single registrations, or the ease with which they could be read or traced, but their material inscription in a book that was venerable in itself and hence never rewritten, reordered, or remade, a mode of recording altogether internal to the religious community and indeed almost an end in itself.

Later necrologies from the Benevento area in southern Italy, in which order seems to dominate every other concern, reveal an entirely different attitude.

The Montecassino necrology in ms Cass. no. 47, compiled in Beneventan minuscule between 1159 and 1166–74 and in use up to the last quarter of the fifteenth century, has the obits rigidly arranged in two columns and in hierarchical order: popes, cardinals, archbishops and bishops, abbots, monks, priests, deacons, subdeacons, simple monks, and lay people. The names of particularly important people are either rubricated on a gold ground or done entirely in capitals. Many hands participated and used very different scripts, Carolingian and Gothic, chancery minuscule and humanist cursive, but they all strove to keep individual obits within the preordained layout.

The necrology of the convent of San Lorenzo, now ms Vat. lat. 5419 (ff. 1r–8v), comes from Benevento itself. It is written in many hands alongside a calendar in Beneventan style, though the recorders of the obits employ other styles. The initial folios down to the middle of folio 2v have been fiercely scraped. The obituaries are of nuns, servants of the convent community, and lay people linked to it in some way. It is a small necrology, the image and product of a restricted community that nevertheless aimed at recording and preserving the memorial patrimony that constituted the guarantee of its relationship with the afterlife, with intercessors and patron saints, protected and favored in their turn by the prayers of the living.

The writing and rewriting of this type of book were always the result of clear and conscious intention. Proof of this, again from Benevento, is the obituary of the collegiate church of Santo Spirito, ordered in 1198 by Abbot Pietro and executed in Beneventan minuscule by Abbot Bartolomeo di San Nicola "Rodenandi," in which it is specified on behalf of its sponsor that "we have had this book made for the redemption of our souls and of all the other brethren and for the remission of all the dead faithful."

The necrology of San Matteo in Salerno, with its several thousand entries, contains a list of people in some way connected with Salerno cathedral (*Liber confratrum*) and a necrology proper (ff. 13r–20v). The obits are laid out in four flanking columns of 45 lines each, with vertical as well as horizontal drypoint ruling. In practice, the records, begun before the end of the eleventh century, continue down to the sixteenth century, though the majority belong to the twelfth and thirteenth centuries. Except for one or two cases (for example in ff. 37r and 38r) where the entries run over into the margin, the many succeeding hands strove to keep the writing within the ruled lines and ensure the graphic harmony and legibility of the text.

But who was it that actually wrote the obits? Undoubtedly members of the religious community, sometime working in turn. Thus, responsibility for writing the work and for its successful outcome impinged on all, and keeping what one may call the "order of the book" was a shared task. Meanwhile, the community that wrote and preserved the book (that curious graveyard of vellum and inscription) was identical with the one that in its daily liturgy performed the celebratory duty, the program and date of which were recorded in the book itself. Was there a link, or did some register the tremor of its possibility, between the dense texture of the recorded entries and the material reality of the cemetery, the tombs, the inscriptions within the community church at least? Probably enough. The circle of commemoration, starting from the death and the dead body of one of the brethren, will have wound its way back in some way.

4.   One of the facets of the cult of the dead in northern Europe (but also in Catalonia) was the prayer association. Several, sometimes widely separated communities might be linked in this way. The main purpose of these associations lay in focusing the members' prayers for mercy on a single dead individual.

This necessarily required that news of the death of the more illustrious and meritorious be passed on in a reasonable time. The material carriers of the news were the so-called "rolls of the dead," scrolls sometimes 20 or 30 yards long consisting of sewn sheets of parchment wrapped around a wooden staff. Though the first extant example dates from 968–77, their use was not especially frequent until the twelfth century. They opened with an encyclical letter from the sender (one of the associated prayer groups) in which the customary greeting was followed by announcement of a death. As the bearer made his rounds, breaking his monthlong or even yearlong journey at this or that monastery, this or that church, the scroll gradually became filled in with declarations of adherence from the religious institutions visited.

These communities did not limit themselves to recording their simple solidarity, but usually solicited prayers for their own dead, either generically or by detailing the names in lists more or less long. Thus, what had begun as a document inviting the commemoration of a single individual changed as it traveled into an obituary compiled by dozens or hundreds of communities that amassed the names of those to be commemorated.

Three hundred and twenty original scrolls have survived, complete or as fragments, the best known of which is that compiled at the French abbey of Savigny (in the diocese of Avranches, in Normandy) for the death of its founder, Blessed Vital, who died on September 16, 1122. Lacking its beginning, it consists of fifteen parchment folios written on the recto and verso and is nine and one-half meters in length. Two hundred and seven communities joined, drawn from a vast area embracing northern France and 25 counties in southern England. The texts added by the various communities visited are extremely variegated and go from simple adherence ("May the soul of the Blessed Vital and those of all the faithful rest in peace. Pray for ours.") to poems, sometimes rhetorically pretentious, sometimes unbelievably playful, sometimes—as with that of the nuns of Fontevrault—painfully misspelled. The graphic aspect also varies considerably, sometimes simple and unadorned, sometimes emphasized by the use of complicated interwoven capitals, complicated ligatures, and ornamental designs.

The scroll of the Blessed Vital, precious from the palaeographic and cultural standpoint, shows that the itinerant message taken around by the monk *portitores* did not restrict itself to a pious liturgical function, but established relationships of deeper mutual awareness and influence, even of a literary kind, between the various linked centers. In some cases, given the sequence of complicated verse texts, it would almost seem that the purpose of common prayer had faded or been forgotten. Nevertheless, the connection with rituals of death and with the names and presence of the dead remained strong, bound fast in a way the writing could not elude.

⁓

5.   Between the end of the tenth century and the first half of the thirteenth, the expressive language of written death in western Europe underwent a series of changes that deeply altered its letter design and layout—the writing, in short, and its spaces.

What principally changed was the script and the way of presenting it. The classicizing and spacious capital of Carolingian origin, which was still being used in Rome for superb archaistic epitaphs, was replaced by a rounded majuscule with letters of uncial type, ligatures between neighboring letters and the inclusion of smaller letters in larger ones, thick strokes, double strokes, and use of fillets and ornamental studs—what, in brief, is commonly known as the Gothic majuscule. But not only was the script different from the models of the past, even the layout of exhibited writing, earlier framed by square or rectangular slabs with the long axis vertical, now began to take on an unframed, rectangular, sideways layout, with a cramped arrangement of lines, of words on the line, and of letters in the words, following what may be called book models. Putting it succinctly, a shift was made from the slab to the page. Meanwhile, during the same period, a further novelty in funerary writing, it, too, lacking any precedent in ancient tradition, was establishing itself in northern Europe, in Germany, France, England, and gradually in Italy also. This was the pavement tombstone, with the writing running thick and unbroken along the external border of the four sides. In this case, the passage was from the slab to the strip, prompted this time not by the book, but by the crafting of small objects, in particular gold working, but also ivory carving, the influence of enamels and fabrics, and even, in all likelihood, that of Scandinavian funerary epigraphy of the Viking age.

Both these new aspects of exhibited writing actually resulted in a considerable reduction of the writing space, in a shrinking in the size of letters, and in a considerable decrease in the legibility of the text. At the same time, in line with a trend already established in the tenth century, the absolute dominance of textuality in funerary epigraphy was broken. Once again, the text was joined by imagery, in particular the effigy of the dead, at first given generic features and later personalized.

These radical if gradual changes in systems of writing death coincided with other phenomena of a more general kind. These included a more widespread literacy than in the past, mainly urban and for the first time since the second century A.D. involving wide strata of the laity and numerous women; a new type of book, the scholastic university volume consisting of text and comment, used for both teaching and reading; and a new type of book hand, generally known as Gothic minuscule. In the more narrowly epigraphic sphere, in Pisa, in Salerno, in Milan and Ferrara, celebratory public inscriptions made a return to the outdoors, to squares and the external surfaces of monuments, and there was a quantitative increase in funerary inscriptions, now also dedicated to the laity, to women, families, and merchants. In cities throughout Europe, the right to written death gradually spread to ever larger sections of the population and was no longer the exclusive privilege of the "great" and the upper clergy. Churches became filled with tombs and funerary inscriptions. The move out into the square of public celebratory epigraphy was matched by the packing of private commemorative epigraphy into the new Gothic churches to an extent difficult to conceive of today. According to Emile Mâle, "one did not walk on the pavement in Notre-Dame in Paris, one walked on slabs of engraved stone or on sheets of brass decorated with funerary effigies."

As Dante put it:

> that there be memory of them,
> tombs in the floor over the buried
> bear incised what they were before. . . .
> (*Purgatorio*, 12, 16–18)

In fact, floor slabs combined the immediate closeness of the body with the dual characterization of writing and a likeness, usually of the deceased lying in the sleep of death, but decked out in all their worldly attributes. The first examples of the genre date from the eleventh century. One that stands out for its unrepeatable (and never repeated) originality happens to be the earliest of them all (after 1048), the tombstone carved for Abbot Isarn of Saint Victor in Marseilles, on which the writing in a large inscribed rectangle covers—indeed, all but takes the place of—the deceased's portrait, only the head and feet of which are shown, surrounded in their turn by two strips of semicircular writing. Then there is the tombstone of Sancho, the great king of Navarre and Castile, executed some time after his death (1035), on which the writing is set around the four edges; and again, the splendid bronze slab of Rudolph of Sweden (d. 1080), where the writing is engraved around the entire edge in a majuscule already containing elements of Gothic, but still well-spaced and readable.

The finest examples of the genre, however, come from the early thirteenth century. It is enough to mention the raised tombstone supported by four lions of Evrard de Fouilly, bishop of Amiens (d. 1222), already fashioned as a monument, and the matchless grace of those of Jean (d. 1248) and Blanche (d. 1243) of France in Saint-Denis, where a strip of writing in red enamel runs around the bas-relief portraits, and the field is filled in with enamels of various colors.

Floor slabs and funerary monuments with recumbent figures were for centuries a characteristic element in the cult of the dead in late Medieval and Renaissance Europe. From the standpoint of this study, however, the main feature of these new and recherché forms of funerary pietàs remained unchanged: the usurpation of the writing (which is sometimes totally absent), by the figure, and the taking over of the letter by the likeness of the deceased.

Monument and Document

1.   In his *Candelabrum eloquentiae* of 1227, Boncompagno da Signa thus described the burials of the "great" in his time:

The tombs of illustrious persons and of the wisest men are frequently adorned like marriage beds; canopies of stone decorated in different colors are constructed, epitaphs are set on them, and poems composed in which posterity is reminded of the greatness and merits of the dead; and they always end with the theme of contempt for the world; images of God, of the Blessed Virgin, or of the male and female saints, in honor of whom the churches are founded, are painted; the angels or the saints that present the souls of the dead to the Divine Majesty are also painted; but once they made marvelous sculptures in choice marbles with abbreviated words that today we no longer can entirely read and understand. In Greece, the tombs of certain emperors are made of pure gold, adorned with precious stones; the tomb of Mahomed the Saracen, who delivered to his followers the law of error, is of Andanic iron; their satraps with unutterable skill and secret calculations set it in their greatest city called Mech in such a way that it stays constantly suspended in the air without visible support. Lately, the people of Rome also built the tomb of Giovanni Capocci on the Capitoline with marvelous construction. Finally, one should remark that there are five things that lead posterity to adorn tombs: custom, devotion, love, the merits of people, and the vain desire for glory.

Boncompagno here gives us a description of the new funerary wall monument in the form of a bed with the dead laid out in the act of sleeping, mounted on a decorated base, surmounted by an architectural structure in the form of a canopy and variously ornamented with figurations and symbols. Here we have an artistic form typical of the Gothic period and proper to Italy—with some precedents in funerary monuments of chest form or erected on pillars—that also recalls the niche burials of the paleo-Christian catacombs.

Boncompagno records the wealth of ornament, the colors, obviously painted or in mosaic, the figurative motifs, the classical and Arab precedents. Of particular interest here are the passages relating to epigraphical texts and to the sole contemporary example explicitly mentioned: "epitaphs are set on them, and poems composed in which posterity is reminded of the greatness and merits of the dead; and they always end with the theme of contempt for the world." Thus Boncompagno describes the presence of exhibited text, distinguishes texts in prose ("epitaphia") and verse ("carmina"), and points out their function of reminding posterity of the greatness and merits of the dead, with the addition of the topos of contempt for the world, in obvious contrast to the grandeur of the tomb and the praise expressed in the epigraphic text.

Boncompagno provides a sole example of the new type of funerary monument that had caught his eye, one close to him in time and evidently seen firsthand, the funerary monument of the Roman senator Giovanni Capocci (d. 1216), erected by the people of Rome (as he puts it) on the Capitoline and no longer extant. It was probably a structure similar to the contemporary monument erected by the Milanese in the Palazzo della Ragione to Oldrado da Tressena, with equestrian images and a verse inscription set on a horizontal plaque and laid out in two columns in handsome, well-spaced Gothic capitals.

2.   In Italy between the first half of the thirteenth century and the second, two opposing trends emerged in the presence and role of the text and of writing in the spatial organization of the new funerary wall monuments. One allowed for a considerable amount of writing, even if in new forms and new patterns of layout, while the other failed to consider it on the level of overall design and inserted it at dead points of the monument, much reducing legibility, and at the limit, preventing the reader or spectator's understanding, if not perception, of it.

Rome was the place where an ancient artistic and craft tradition, the "cosmateque" skills of the local marble workers, made a very large contribution to the definition of the new type of monument, and where an artist like Arnolfo di Cambio, whose education and culture were completely different from those of the Roman tradition, created some of his masterpieces in this field.

This all came about in the specific arc of time between the second half of the thirteenth century and the early years of the fourteenth century, when, according to Richard Krautheimer, "a series of decidedly Roman popes strove to restore to the city the role of *caput mundi* it had had at the start of the century, but without success, because the political and economic reality remained much below that of the grandiose image. Despite this, during that period, the city became the cultural capital of Italy, if not of the world, and the center of a new art." A political and cultural project of this scale and scope not only required a series of highly capable popes, but depended for its success on cultivated members of the Curia who were ambitious and greedy for power and glory, and on cardinals just as forceful, but also rich and powerful. All these people, and the intellectual and artistic milieus that served them, perceived in the new, large, wall funerary monument the instrument of a program of glorification of the Church of Rome through magnification of its representatives on earth, popes, cardinals, and the prelates of the Roman Curia. According to Herklotz, "the wall tomb with statue of the dead can be interpreted as a specifically ecclesiastic creation."

The celebratory process employed a precise iconographic program centering on a realistic and hence recognizable likeness of the dead, on his solemn and official portrayal as a sleeping potentate. It required the elevation of his body and of his double—the portrait—above the ground, and by giving it a central setting in the monumental complex, it relegated the surrounding iconographic motifs, whether saints or the Virgin, to a subordinate position. Spaces were strictly allocated and writing was reduced so as not to disturb the balanced alternation of figural motifs, but especially to prevent the spectator's eye being drawn away from the *monument* to the *document*, from the effigy itself, eloquent not least because realistic, to the text.

Nevertheless, the text remained. The text remained on the level of a documentary declaration imbued with authenticity, as biographical explication, sometimes even as acknowledgment of its creator, and as Boncompagno says, as a proclamation of greatness. In short, it survived as caption, often compressed into a horizontal rectangle or in strips crammed with script and abbreviations, barely visible and hardly readable. Despite this, in certain cases for which the workshops of the Roman marble craftsmen were responsible, the text manages, even in its modern layout and *mise en écrit*, to hold on to its own space of display, its own orderly spaciousness, and an overall legibility.

〜

3.   Surviving evidence of what took place in Rome is often barely understandable on account of destruction and displacement and the alterations carried out over time. Some creations—the written documentation of which has survived—do stand out, however, and help shed light on the situation of conflict and expressive difficulty already mentioned.

The large funerary wall monument in San Lorenzo of Cardinal Guglielmo Fieschi (d. 1256), reconstructed after the damage of the last war, bears two inscriptions, one a mere caption on the cornice of the sarcophagus and practically illegible, the other laid out in seven lines on a large rectangular slab set—if the modern placing is correct—between the fresco and the antique sarcophagus containing the body. The graphic typology (Romanesque-Gothic capitals) and the spacing of letters and lines make the verse text sufficiently legible.

By contrast, the large epigraph (how or where set we do not know) from the Orvieto monument to Cardinal Guillaume de Braye (d. 1282), signed by Arnolfo di Cambio, is in twelve lines of cramped Gothic capitals so packed with abbreviations as to make any attempt at reading arduous, even from relatively close up. The epigraph in Saint John Lateran, obviously "Roman" in execution and tradition, on the monument—again by Arnolfo—of the papal notary Riccardo Annibaldi (d. 1289) is quite different. The Romanesque-Gothic majuscule is well spaced, with very few abbreviations, large, clearly visible, and easily readable.

A true grasp of the phenomenon requires that one set it in a broader perspective. One needs to takes account of the fact that funerary inscriptions belong to a more general category of written product—epigraphy—that is, exhibited writing. And one must remember that the modes of exhibition changed very considerably during the Gothic period in terms of *mise en page, mise en écrit,* and degree of legibility. Within a very few decades, exhibited writing changed in formulation and layout from epigraphy to caption, lost its centrality, and became marginal, and instead of being a finished product, valid in itself, it became an appendage, conceived, designed, executed, and set up as a function of something else.

Though the reasons for the change were both graphic and ideological, a certain role was undoubtedly played by the artist, as certain of the examples mentioned clearly show. Indeed, between the twelfth and thirteenth centuries, architectural and sculptural products ever more frequently bore the Latin signature of their creator or creators in a visible position, sometimes alone, sometimes with the name of the patron. This fact is important in itself. For the first time since the classical age, the artist was rediscovered and acknowledged as the creator and protagonist of an event considered memorable. But it is also important in terms of graphic exhibition, both because artists' signatures are to be seen as "captions" and because, on each occasion, it was necessary to pick out suitable writing spaces for them—very often having the form of a strip—within the spatial complex of the work.

4. According to Boncompagno's account, the funerary monument was (in the absolute, *is*) a monument to "memory," the purpose of which was an everlasting record of one of the "great" dead, his family, and social role. On occasion, the living, patrons and artists, desired to become part of the memorial by linking their own names to that of the person celebrated. And this they did not so much by invading the plane of representation—which was normally kept for the dead and the theater of his celebration—but that of writing, which was, as I have said, complementary in function, but which also had power to authenticate. If it was not a "monument," it was at least a "document."

The funerary "wall" monument (or those standing alone in space) represented an important cultural phenomenon of self-celebration by the governing ecclesiastical aristocracy, which was soon taken up by the "great" laity also. To mention only Italian examples, the imposing funerary monuments of the Scaligeri in Verona are of great importance. Isolated (no longer attached to the wall) and set up in the open air, in the urban spaces of the capital city of the state (and no longer in the confines of the churches), they represent a great element of novelty for that very reason. The writing, which plays a documentary and celebratory role of noteworthy importance, is set low, in a position to guarantee legibility, despite the thicket of Gothic graphic typology and layout. The monument to Cangrande della Scala (d. 1329) is a classical and well-known example. The slab with epigraph is set below the sarcophagus, itself in the lowest section of the canopy, at a dizzying distance from the summit of the startling pyramid from which the illustrious dead sneers harshly down.

The inscription on the large funerary monument executed in Pisa by Tino di Camaino for the emperor Henry VII, now in fragments, was probably also meant to be set low. Other examples, all from the fourteenth century, reveal different attempts at solving the question of placement, for which the structure of the funerary monument (highly compact even in its complex structure) seems to have left insufficient space.

Thus, for example, in the funerary monument of Ranieri Ubertini, bishop of Cortona (d. 1348), the three-line inscription is inserted oddly into the drum of the canopy. Despite its curious position, it remains to some degree legible. Another monument attributed to Tino di Camaino, executed for Enrico di Sanseverino (d. 1336), in the church of Santa Maria Maggiore di Teggiano, has a packed inscription incongruously set on the upper and side edges of the sarcophagus, difficult to decipher, given its dense layout and small letter size.

5.   In reality, every aspect of the funerary wall monument was new and therefore important, as it is also important that the space destined for writing diminished, while the monumental area increased in size. If one calculates the ratio between the overall surface of a monument and the exhibited writing, one rapidly realizes the degree of compression suffered by writing in the design of the funerary record in Gothic Europe. In less extreme form, the same thing happened in the classicizing examples of the Roman marble masons.

It was not only a matter of compression, but of a decrease in autonomy (the abolition of frame), of visual displacement, of textual density, of an abundance of compression, and of an excessive clustering of letters. The general result was a progressive decrease in legibility. It is certainly no accident that the funerary inscriptions (like the general epigraphic products of the period) show an ever growing number of abbreviations, and that this progressive increase occurs more in non-Roman examples like the de Braye monument in Orvieto than in examples of a more properly "Roman" tradition, such as those by Giovanni di Cosma.

In short, one may say that while in Romanesque and late Romanesque funerary epigraphy up to the end of the eleventh century legibility was positively sought for, in funerary epigraphy of the Gothic period, and particularly in that of the great funerary monuments of the thirteenth and even fourteenth centuries, legibility was no longer thought of as a primary goal if not within narrow limits. The exhibited text had to remain visible to all, but readable only to some, to those few who desired or had to do so. There is an exact parallel here with documentary records.

The ideological message of the monument was in fact left to the complex of images, to the likeness, to the coats of arms, that all visitors and all the faithful could at least on a surface level comprehend and decipher, even from a distance. The reading of a text for information and authentication could be left to occasions of deliberate investigation, study, or meditation, all of which entailed close physical inspection of the inscribed space or spaces according to procedures analogous to those employed in identifying a relic, where a text remained linked to the sacred object solely for the purpose of documenting its nature and authenticity in case of inspection and verification.

The title of this chapter is a slightly modified version of Jacques Le Goff's statement that every "document" was a "monument" during the Middle Ages. One could justly say, for the purposes of this study, that every "monument" was also a "document" in which exhibited writing performed the complementary but juridically and culturally essential function of authentication and commentary on the ideological message transmitted by the figured complex. Though compressed and marginal, it always remained visibly displayed for all—almost a paratext, necessary, but independent and complementary, in regard to an iconographic text totally autonomous in its meaningful entirety.

1. Slab with nine names from the small burial ground of Sellàda. Athens, Epigraphic Museum.

2. Stele of Dermis and Kittilos of Tanagra, ca. 600 B.C. Athens, National Museum.

3. Stele of Avile Tite. Florence, Archaeological Museum.

4. Stele of Filo and Megakles, 540–535 B.C. New York, Metropolitan Museum of Art.

5. Burial stele of Phrasikleia, 530–525 B.C. Athens, National Museum.

6. Stele of Archeos of Melos, fifth century B.C. Melos Museum.

7. Inscription in honor of Caius Poplicius Bibulus, first century B.C. Rome, Piazza Venezia.

8. Stele of Democleides, fourth century B.C. Athens, National Museum.

9. Sarcophagus of Lucius Scipio Barbatus, ca. 298 B.C. Vatican City, Vatican Museums. (Photo: Alinari, Florence)

10. Grave slab of Potitus Valerius Messalla, 10–12 A.D. Rome, National Roman Museum.

11. Funerary monument of Marcus Vergilius Eurysaces, first century B.C. Rome, Porta Maggiore. (Photo: Maria Teresa Natale, Rome)

12. Stele of Publius Longidienus, shipwright, first century A.D. Ravenna, National Museum.

13. Funerary stele of the *miles* Marcus Braetius of the XIII Gemina legion, 9–17 A.D. Mannheim Museum.

14. Slab of Agapis, from the cemetery of Ottavilla. Rome, Lateran Epigraphic Museum.

15. Epitaph of Titus Eupor, from the cemetery of Pretestato. Rome, Lateran Epigraphic Museum.

16. Overall view of the basilica of Candidus. Haïdra (Tunisia).

17. Epitaph of Bishop Melleus. Haïdra (Tunisia).

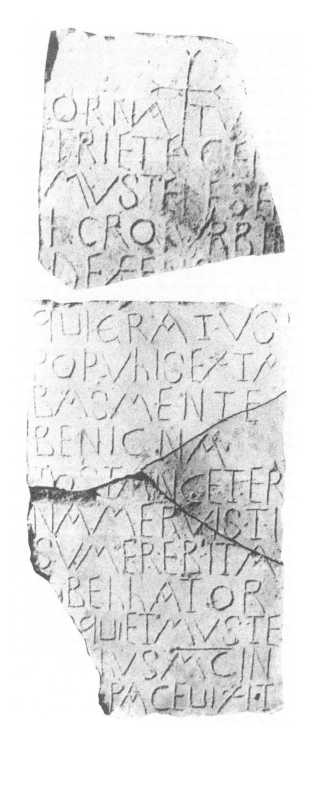

18. Epitaph of Mustelus. Haïdra (Tunisia).

19. Epitaph of Bernardus. Toulouse, Musée des Augustins.

20. Epitaph of Pope Hadrian I. Rome, Saint Peter's, porch.

21. MS Vat. lat. 5419, f. 5*v*, Vatican Library. Vatican City (Vatican Library photo).

22. Scroll of Blessed Vital. Paris, National Archives.

23. Obelisk of King Gorm and Queen Tyra. Jellinge, Jutland.

24. Funerary wall monument of Cardinal Guglielmo Fieschi. Rome, San Lorenzo.

25. Arnolfo di Cambio, funerary wall monument of Cardinal Guillaume de Braye. Orvieto, San Domenico.

26. Funerary monument to Rolandino de' Passeggeri (d. 1250). Bologna, Piazza San Domenico.

27. Monumental tomb of Cangrande della Scala. Verona. (Photo: Alinari, Florence)

28. Funerary ark of Giovanni d'Andrea (d. 1348), detail. Bologna, City Medieval Museum.

29. Funerary monument of Lovato Lovati, before 1309. Padua, Piazza Antenore.

30. Funerary monument of Rolando da Piazzola. Padua, Piazza del Santo.

31. Funerary wall monument for the antipope John
XXIII. Florence, Baptistery.

32. Bernardo Rossellino, funerary wall monument of Leonardo
Bruni, 1449–51. Florence, Santa Croce.

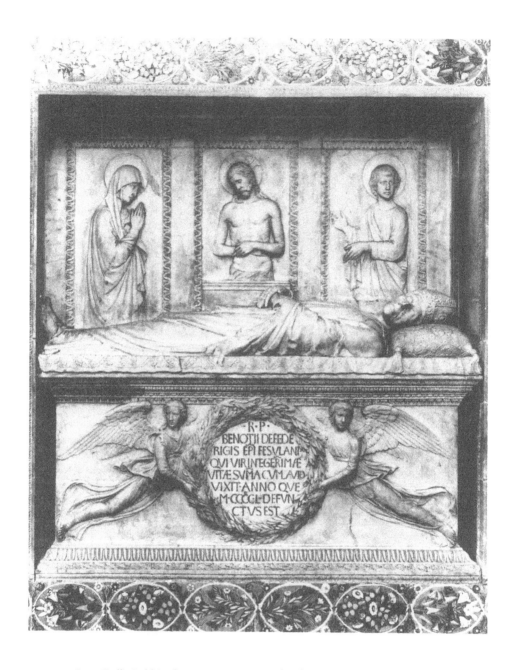

R·P·
BENOTII DEFEDE
RIGIS EPI FESVLANI
QVI VIR INTEGERIMÆ
VITÆ SVMA CVM LAVD
VIXIT·ANNO QVE
M·CCCCL·DEFVN
CTVS EST

33. Luca Della Robbia, funerary monument of Bishop Benozzo Federighi. Florence, Santa Trinita.

34. Andrea del Verrocchio, joint tomb of Piero and Giovanni de' Medici. Florence, San Lorenzo.

35. Sassetti chapel. Florence, Santa
     Trinita.

36. Antonio del Pollaiolo, funerary
     monument of Sixtus IV. Rome,
     Saint Peter's.

37. Autograph jotting by Michelangelo, sheet F 9 A. London, British Museum.

38. Michele Sammicheli, tomb of Pietro Bembo. Padua, Sant'Antonio.

39. Tomb of Giovanni Francesco Vegio. Pisa, Camposanto.

40. S. Rybisch and T. Fendt,
    Monumenta, Frankfurt 1589,
    title page.

41. S. Rybisch and T. Fendt,
    Monumenta, Frankfurt 1589,
    plate 10.

42. Etching in P. Della Valle, *Relazione* . . . , Rome 1627.

43. Funerary monument of Christoph von Freiberg (d. 1690). Augsburg Cathedral.

44. Gian Lorenzo Bernini, funerary monument of Urban VIII. Rome, Saint Peter's.

45. Gian Lorenzo Bernini, De Silva funerary monument. Rome, Sant'Isidoro.

46. Triple gravestone of the Cutler children, 1680. Charlestown, Massachusetts, cemetery. (Photo: Newberry Library, Chicago)

47. Gravestone of Ruth Carter, 1697–98. Granary, Massachusetts, cemetery. (Photo: Newberry Library, Chicago)

48. N. Lamson, gravestone of the Reverend Jonathan Pierpont, 1709. Wakefield, Massachusetts, cemetery. (Photo: Newberry Library, Chicago)

49. Gravestone of Doctor
Herbert Mann, 1778. North
Attleborough, Massachusetts,
cemetery. (Photo: Newberry
Library, Chicago)

50. Gravestone of Thomas Hurd,
1784. Granary, Massachusetts,
cemetery. (Photo: Newberry
Library, Chicago)

51. Tommaso Righi, funerary monument of C. Pio Balestra, 1776. Rome,
Santi Luca e Martina.

52. Antonio Canova, funerary monument of
Clement XIV, 1787. Rome, Santi Apostoli.

53. Antonio Canova, funerary monument of
Giacomo Volpato, 1807. Rome, Santi
Apostoli.

54. Nineteenth-century view of Le Père Lachaise cemetery in Paris.

55. View of the war cemetery of Redipuglia.

56. View of the cemetery of Staglieno in Genoa. (Photo: Alinari, Florence)

57. Page of the *Frankischer Tag*, with death notices.

58. Photo of death posters in Isernia.

59. "Holy pictures."

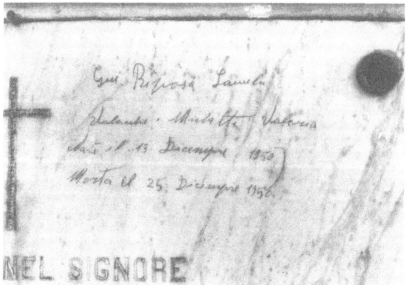

60. Tombstone in the cemetery of Vetralla (Viterbo). (Photo: Carlo Tedeschi)

61. Tombstone in the cemetery of Montefortino (Ascoli Piceno).
(Photo: Carlo Tedeschi)

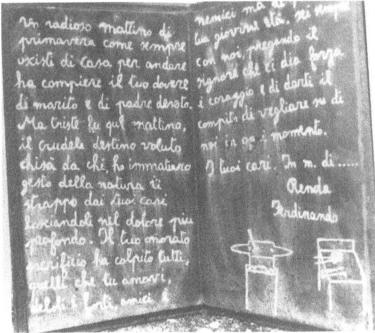

62. Tombstone in the cemetery of Castel Sant'Elia. (Photo: Carlo Tedeschi)

63. Tomb of F. Renda, Calabria (precise whereabouts unknown).

64. Funerary monument of Jim Morrison (d. 1971). Paris, Le Père Lachaise cemetery.

The Body, Knowledge, and Money

1.   The thirteenth century in Europe was the century of the university, though it would perhaps be better to say it was the century of the professors. It was in fact then, in that shifting social panorama, that the figure of the cultured layman first appeared and established itself: a person who lived by his own work, and whose work was that of teaching in those free institutions capable of bestowing the *licentia docendi* in certain disciplinary fields, institutions that today we call universities and that in the Middle Ages had very different structures from place to place and different modes of government and of functioning.

The university professor constitutes the model of the new, late medieval intellectual. He created, and at the same time used, the primary instrument of written culture, the book, and he bent it to the needs of his task, transforming its aspect and making it functional to the *lectio*, the reading of a commentated text. He and his like formed the new elites of culture and religion, in politics, in law, and in the healing of bodies, and made their function indispensable to the creation of the new princely states, of the new bureaucratically organized kingdoms. He aspired to be considered part of the aristocracy that ruled states and money. He enriched himself, adopted a noble lifestyle, dressed in a costly and characteristic way, gave his job as teacher a particularly solemn liturgy, elevated himself in the exercise of his functions above the audience of students by "reading" from a high and imposing cathedra. All this was allowed him because his function was acknowledged as socially useful to those who exerted power, and useful also to the city that had the privilege of lodging a university, a center of attraction for young men, and an institution that was a source of prestige, trade, wealth, and renown for all citizens. Thus, almost naturally, a new and ideal aristocracy of "heroes" of knowledge, whose example had to be recorded and kept alive after their deaths, became identified in the great teachers. Their works, the texts handed on and copied time and time again, survived in the activity of disciples, in the reading of students, in the care of libraries. And it was considered proper to reinforce the esteem in which the names and function of the greatest were held by also publicly honoring their remains as if they were sovereigns or great prelates, or deserving of the gratitude of the whole community. And in the belief that they would enjoy some reflected glory, their physical heirs and disciples, often their successors in honors and offices, took a direct part in this work of interested pietàs, in the creation of this funerary cult of a new type.

Very soon the professors of the Studio in Bologna began to enjoy solemn funerary memorials. As early as 1178, Guglielmo da Lucca, reader in philosophy, was buried in San Pietro and had an epitaph in elegiac couplets set on a fine rectangular tombstone. Twenty years later, in 1197, the eminent jurist Giovanni Bassiano was buried in the same church and rewarded by an analogous epitaph in hexameters, laid out, on the book model, in two columns of regular Gothic capitals. And it was again in Bologna that in the second half of the thirteenth century the custom began of lodging the remains of some of the great teachers from the local university in solemn outdoor monuments close to famous churches.

The chosen model was a structure that, like the wall monuments of great churchmen, raised the mortal remains of the dead above the ground, a structure that would thus symbolize, not least by its isolation in the open, the superiority of the aristocracy of knowledge, just as in the liturgy of the *lectio*, the raised position of the cathedra confirmed it in daily practice. The body, placed in an ark of stone, was set in a pillared structure, often with a double order, topped by a pyramid. The solution was entirely new, even if the imposing height and the peaked summit vaguely recall the Romanesque-Gothic ciboria, and certainly impressed its contemporaries. In his *Historia universalis*, Riccobaldo da Ferrara speaks highly of the monumental tombs of Odofredo and of Accursio: "These two are buried in Bologna in the church of the Friars Minor; over their tombs were erected two fine pyramids to roof the mausoleum." In fact the two great jurists, Odofredo (d. 1265) and Accursio (d. 1263), and the latter's son and successor, Francesco (d. 1293), were among the first Bolognese professors to have funerary monuments, all three close to San Francesco. The others include that of Egidio dei Foscherari (d. 1289), close to San Domenico, and the famous one of Rolandino dei Passeggeri (d. 1300), in Piazza San Domenico. All were more or less radically altered, both at the end of the nineteenth century and after the disastrous bombing of 1943, and we do not know the exact location and extent of the inscribed portion for any of them. The impression given by the placing and the crammed layout of the surviving writing is that of a record of celebration and remembrance that hardly lends itself to easy public reading. In contrast, the later ark of Giovanni d'Andrea (d. 1348), once in San Domenico and now in the Medieval Museum of Bologna, has an ample, well-spaced inscription set low, in large and readable Gothic capitals. This is also the case with other funerary epigraphs for Bolognese professors not on individual pyramidal monuments and all from the first half of the fourteenth century, where there is always a bas-relief scene with the topos of the *lectio* parallel with the inscription. The tombstone "in the fashion for a scholar," as a Bolognese notary expressed it in 1372, was not exclusive to the city. It appeared simultaneously outside of Italy to commemorate the figure of the new European intellectual with the honor he deserved.

2.   During the thirteenth century, first in Tuscany, then throughout Italy, and finally in the rest of Europe, a new figure of the writer, appeared and became active. This was the merchant who kept his own accounts of the income and expenditures of the commercial enterprises in which he was involved, recorded purchases and sales, and listed and described his property. He also wrote letters to partners and colleagues to keep them up to date, took note of what interested him, gathered news of his family and the community to which he belonged, and set down the events in which he was involved or of which he knew. In short, no matter what else he did, he was always writing, intent on leaving some trace or record, as a check, for purposes of comparison, but also so as to remember better and better remind others. It was no personal whim that moved Giovanni Morelli to tell his son to keep written note of every activity: "See to it that what you do is set out at length in your books, and never spare your pen, and make your meaning clear in the book." And Leon Battista Alberti considered that it was "the task of the merchant and every craftsman who has to deal with

several people, always to write everything, every contract, every entry into and exit from the workshop, and thus almost always to have pen in hand, since often checking everything," and in consequence "always to have ink-stained hands."

A large part of the written production of the merchants was thus essentially of a mnemonic kind. This is particularly true of the books of "remembrance" or "of the family," in which the family head recorded his economic and biographical vicissitudes and those of the group to which he belonged, a group understood both in the broad sense of a joint venture and in the narrow sense of a line of direct descent.

In these works, compiled by family heads over several generations, sometimes for more than a century, amid news of births, weddings, major events in the life of each member of the group, and the growth of the family property, come reports of death, set down like all the rest in their proper place in a general chronological order that was usually scrupulously respected. This is especially the case with the more complex and detailed exemplars from the fourteenth and fifteenth centuries, centuries in which, after the funerary inscription and the ecclesiastical necrology, the registration of dead found a fresh location and another system of writing, the record book of the bourgeoisie, archive of economic fact and family register at the same time.

The style of the record book, generally dry and sober, did not lend itself to bursts of feeling; hence, the registering of death was usually short and terse, often enriched with details of an economic kind relating to the reversion of dowries or to wills and the consequent division of property among heirs. But the chronological setting of the event is always specified with the greatest accuracy; sometimes even the hour is given. Details of the burial are set down, sometimes the fatal sickness mentioned. The formula most frequently used to introduce the individual necrology is: "God called him (or her) to Himself," with variants: "as please God . . . God called her to Himself, or "it pleased God to call to Himself." Further information sometimes given constitutes a reminder to the descendants meant to render the funerary cult more vital, the presence of the dead in daily life, the gnomic and exemplary value of their life experience more alive and vivid:

And God called her to Himself on the 11th of February in the year 1397 and she was sick 7 months with different maladies and her memory was almost lacking because of this very great malady.   (Matteo Corsini)

Then, as it pleased God, God called the said lady Salvagia to Himself on the 13th day of February 1409 at 9½ of the clock and the sickness was that she fell being great with a boy child, that she carried 38 days after the fall and she made the boy in right fashion. . . . May God grant her true forgiveness that great harm it was for she was a most excellent woman.   (Giovanni Corsini)

The record of the burial place constituted an important element in the cult. Thus, Giovanni Morelli records that of his beloved sister Bartolomea in Santa Croce:

As you enter under the vaults, after a door, go into a cemetery shaped like a room, and it is on the right hand, as you go through the said door, along the wall.

I have wanted to make it clear in this way because seeing her burial place for her bounty to all of us there come odor [of sanctity] from her and from the place where her bones are.

The differences between the ecclesiastical necrologies already mentioned and the merchant records of death are naturally many and deep. First, there is the fact that the latter are set in a context, and only within it do they fulfill their memorial function, whereas the necrologies do so autonomously. Then, there is the relationship with time. For the necrologies, this is the altogether relative one of the liturgy, while for the merchants, it is the absolute one of human affairs, or better, as Alberti puts it, "the season of doing." Finally, there is the formulation of the record. In the discourse of the merchants, this is in the vernacular and employs the formulas of a popular piety that the ecclesiastical necrology, always written in Latin, naturally ignores. This does not mean, however, that there was not a common wish to provide the community with a memorial instrument capable of ordering the cult through the written registration of the individual date of death. Though following different schemes, they were both internally consistent and shared the material but important feature of being set down in books. In many cases, perhaps in all, this constituted a second and separate inscription of the funerary record after that on stone linked to the burial place.

3.   While Bologna honored the heroes of the new aristocracy of knowledge "in modern fashion," in Padua, the nucleus of another and different intellectual aristocracy, that of nascent Venetian Humanism,

looked to the past for "ancient" models, venerable for their age and cultural prestige.

As we know, a tombstone from the Roman period was discovered in Padua in the first half of the thirteenth century that was wrongly believed to belong to Livy. Writing just a little later, Lovato Lovati could say: "And today in Padua, one sees his tomb of stone in the monastery of Santa Giustina." In 1284, one was found, again in Padua, that in all probability Lovato himself wanted to believe, and certainly got others to believe, contained the remains of Antenor, the mythical founder of the city. He composed and got affixed two plaques written in round, well-spaced Gothic capitals, with strongly contrasting thick and thin strokes and ornamental elements, extremely elegant in their layout and forms. These uncertain (and false) incunabula gave rise to a cultural enterprise that barely two centuries later was to see the rebirth of an epigraphy formally modeled on the classical one of the Golden Age. At the time, in the Padua of Albertino Mussato and his colleagues, there was still a long way to go. The models had, however, been identified, and around them began a long-lasting game, rich in misunderstandings and in partial imitations, in enthusiasms and ignorance, in restoration and repudiation.

At the dawn of the new century, Lovato Lovati had a "modern" funerary monument built for himself in the form of an ark—but was not that of the alleged Antenor an ark also! He had attached to it as many as four inscriptions: a title, two couplets, and a date—completed obviously after his death. It was in substance a medieval burial complex. However, though the script is a normal Gothic capital, certain formulas ("V.F." and "D.M.") recall classical models.

The ambiguous oscillation between the charm of the ancient and the prestige of the "modern" can again be seen in the tomb monument built—according to a formula taken from the epitaph of the pseudo Livy—"both for him and his," by Lovato's nephew, Rinaldo da Piazzola, in Padua itself. A Roman sarcophagus was transformed into an ark, described as "mausoleum" and "sarcophagum," and a splendid and extremely legible plaque in large Gothic capitals, dedicated to his son Guido, was set up in plain sight, while his other children, Rolando and Aicarda, are recorded lower down.

From Lovato and his milieu of enthusiastic apprentices to Petrarch, the great restorer of knowledge and texts, who in *De remediis utriusque fortune* pours scorn on the new rich, with their pretensions to solemn tombs decorated with statues, a dignity once reserved only to the truly meritorious: "Statues were once the badge of virtue. . . . They were set up to those who had done great deeds or had undergone death for the republic. . . . They were set up to clever and learned men . . . now they are set up at great expense in fine marble to great merchants." Solemn tombs were thus to be kept for those who had earned merit by death in battle, by deeds of public importance, and for wisdom, not for wealth. As he often does, Petrarch here manages to wed the myths of antique and contemporary custom, the heroes and sages of the ancient world and the rulers, the feudal lords, the professors, of his time. As we know, Petrarch also composed a variety of epitaphs. Two plaques recording his beloved grandchild Francescuolo, who died an untimely death in 1368, still exist in Pavia. According to what he says in a consolatory epistle addressed to Donato Albanzani, he oversaw the execution and setting up of at least the larger of the two: "I myself ordered the marble tomb of that child in the city of Pavia inscribed with six elegiac couplets limned in gold letters" (*Seniles*, 10, 4). One of the inscriptions, in couplets as he said, is long and commemorative; the other, for the tombstone, is purely informative. Both are very modern in their well-spaced, large, and legible Gothic capitals, but heavy with decoration and fillets, in the layout, in the end marks of lines, in the now vanished gilding. What strikes one, however, in them as in the Paduan mausoleum of Rolando da Piazzola, is the emphasis on the written text, the centrality claimed by the writing, and its full visibility.

If Petrarch did not restore tomb letter design "all'antica," no more did Coluccio Salutati—his greatest, though indirect, disciple and intellectual successor in the Humanist restoration—wish or know how to do so. We have two of the latter's verse epitaphs, both fashioned for illustrious members of the Corsini family of Florence, the jurist Tommaso and the beatified Neri. Both are similarly positioned in the center of their respective wall monuments and have "modern" layout in two columns of elegant and shapely Gothic capitals, but they betray an equally decided taste for heavy contemporary graphic ornament and artifice.

4.   For many reasons, ways of honoring and remembering the dead of late medieval Europe in writing took many different forms. Take, for example, the introduction of the motif of the book into the icono-

graphic apparatus of the tomb. Though its features and the manner of its appearance differ from case to case and from area to area, it occurs with great regularity.

Often, as in France, Germany, and Spain, it is shown, small in format, in the hands of recumbent queens and great ladies, open to allow for reading and symbolizing edifying sessions spent with books of hours. Sometimes, on the contrary, large and imposing in a stiff binding heavy with studs and clasps, it appears on the tombs of professors and scholars to signify the learning that imbued the life of the dead man and to which he remains physically linked, even after his death, a sealed treasure to which he had the key.

But the book, the common tool of the professors and Humanists, of old and new readers, could not on its own soothe the disquiet of an age in which war and epidemic made death a close neighbor. The cruel slaughter of the Black Death in the years 1347–52—mentioned not least in the *Decameron*—devastated the cities and countryside of Europe and prompted a sterner view of death and a more tragic vision of life itself, leading, for example, to family tombs being brought together in churches, under the direct protection of the saints, and to an abundance of pious and charitable bequests. The Humanism of Petrarch, and more especially that of men like Salutati, was threaded with a vein of ascetic pessimism, loaded with negative considerations on the frailty of human life.

In Italy, the anguish of the intellectual elites at least resolved itself into an attempt to revitalize funerary forms that had disappeared for a millennium and more. In France, in Germany, and in England, it led in quite the opposite direction, to the disturbing creation of what is known as the *transi* tomb, on which the dead is portrayed as a naked, decaying corpse, sometimes with large, repulsive worms battening on its face, legs, and chest.

This phenomenon lasted down to the eighteenth century, when it finally faded out, and I will come back later to its relationship with funerary writing. Here, let me just observe that it appeared in the first half of the fourteenth century, spread rapidly through the regions of northern and central Europe, and ended by rawly pitting the putrefying image of the dead against the glorification and reassurance of Italian funerary epigraphy, the representation of the fact against the written word.

Florence and Rome

1. Between 1425 and 1428, Donatello and Michelozzo, both Florentines, built an imposing tomb monument in the Baptistery of Florence for the antipope, John XXIII, who had died on December 22, 1419. The work, of great political significance, since the Florentine regime had been one of the main supporters of the deposed pope, was commissioned by the dead man's four testamentary executors, among them Giovanni di Bicci de' Medici, who actually financed it, probably for reasons of family prestige. It was the only tomb in a building sacred to the history and memory of the Florentines and the only papal tomb in Florence.

   The model chosen was that of the wall monument proper to the Roman ecclesiastical tradition of the Gothic period, but the fashioning was highly innovative in several respects, in particular the placing and function of writing on it. Set between two ancient pillars, which ennoble and isolate it, the monument is divided into several horizontal levels. The center is occupied by the sarcophagus, with a bronze likeness of the dead man recumbent on it. A large scroll supported by two putti spans the width of the sarcophagus. The simple inscription stands out in four lines of large capitals of a new type, though clearly Romanesque in inspiration:

JOHN, ONCE POPE,
XXIII, DIED IN FLORENCE IN
THE YEAR OF THE LORD 1419, ELEVEN DAYS
BEFORE THE FIRST DAY OF JANUARY.

In virtue of its setting, the inscription constitutes the true center of vision of the monument. The size of the letters makes it visible, and hence readable, from a distance. Though it is in Latin, the sobriety and simplicity of the text make for immediate intelligibility, and legibility and understanding are undoubtedly increased by its visibility and the distinct forms of the letters.

The result is an outstanding reaffirmation of the primacy of writing and its essential indicative function in a complex formal structure of large dimensions. But what is the script used? And why did Donatello and Michelozzo prefer these capitals of Romanesque type to the traditional Gothic capital, so much more artfully ornate and linked for centuries by then to epigraphic practice and to funerary epigraphy in particular?

Since 1366, when Petrarch expressed (*Familiares*, 23, 19, 8) strong criticism to Boccaccio of the poor legibility of the Gothic script of his time and great praise for the clarity and simplicity of an ideal script—obviously corresponding to the Caroline minuscule of the Romanesque period—70 years had passed, and there had been many upheavals in culture and taste. It was in the Florence of Donatello and of Michelozzo, between the end of the fourteenth century and the early years of the fifteenth century, that the rich "dilettante" Niccolò Niccoli and the youthful notary Poggio Bracciolini proposed "the antique" script of eleventh-century and twelfth-century Tuscan manuscripts as a book hand and the Romanesque capitals of manuscripts and monuments of the same period as ornamental capitals. Niccoli was a recreator and restorer of genius and commitment, and he managed to make and procure the making of codices that resembled his models from three or four centuries before "to the life," not just in script, but even in material, in format, and in ornament. He became the center of a movement of young enthusiasts intent on imitating every aspect of the antique—or what they took as such—from the orthography to the artistic forms of texts.

Brunelleschi, Donatello, and Ghiberti heeded him. According to Vespasiano da Bisticci, Niccoli "lent them very great favor in their exertions." It is hence probable that his promptings resulted in the adoption for the monument of John XXIII of a new-old script (even if without the explicitation of the diphthongs), until then present only in the codices, but capable of embodying those criteria of harmony and balance at the basis of the renewal "all'antica" of the artistic forms and taste of the period. It was no accident that Lorenzo Ghiberti used writing as the critical element for explicating the principles of the new style: "likewise, writing is beautiful only when its letters are proportional in shape and size and in placing and in order and in all the visible ways in which all the different parts come together with them." Those years, the third decade of the fifteenth century, were decisive for the definitive establishment of the new Humanist graphic styles then widespread—though in different stylizations—throughout a good part of central and northern Italy. The advent in epigraphy of the "antique" Florentine capital, even with the ambiguous choice of the Romanesque, rather than classical model, marked an important stage in the rejection initiated by the early Florentine Humanists of the "modern"—that is, Gothic—graphic canon. From then onward, despite residual resistance, the graphic language of written death in Italy was to be different from the past and was to follow tendencies in taste destined to remain in force for centuries.

2.   The monument of John XXIII had very strong and immediate influence on the uses of funerary writing in Florence (and Italy) during the second and third quarters of the fifteenth century, not least because it was precisely in that period that Italian Humanists such as Pietro Paolo Vergerio, Barzizza, and Poggio were changing the model for celebration of the illustrious dead and reproposing the literary genre of the public funerary oration in classicizing rhetorical and linguistic forms, thus also contributing to the rejection of the traditional formal modes that had accompanied and informed the celebratory rituality of death in that sphere up until then.

As for Donatello, he almost always succeeded in renewing the old forms of expression by modifying them "all'antica." Between 1428 and 1430, he made a pavement tombstone in Siena for Giovanni Pecci (d. 1426), bishop of Grosseto, in which he exploited the perspective effect from below that informs the whole work. Instead of setting the writing around the four edges, according to the dictates of Gothic tradition, he concentrated it masterfully on a scroll held open by two putti at the foot of the deceased. Though entirely new in arrangement and layout, this inscription is also in "Florentine" Romanesque capitals, but in another hand from that of the funerary monument to John XXIII. So, too, the anonymous slab of Pope Martin V in Saint John Lateran in Rome, modeled on Donatello's, has an inscription on a tabella ansata at the foot of the deceased, carved in a Romanesque kind of capital, though certainly not in the Florentine style.

The tomb of John XXIII acted naturally as model for the analogous wall monuments that characterized large Florentine funerary sculpture for some decades afterward. In many of them, the inscription is given deliberate emphasis by being set in a privileged space.

The large and important funerary monument to Leonardo Bruni (d. 1444) in Santa Croce, fashioned between 1449 and 1452 by Bernardo Rossellino, incorporates a considerable innovation, a rounded arch—embracing and setting off the whole work—that serves once again to highlight the inscription. This, in Florentine capitals on a scroll supported by two putti, is placed low on the sarcophagus, where it stands out almost as a conceptual and exhibited resolution of the semicircular movement shaping the whole structure. The importance attributed to the display of writing in the funerary space is also confirmed by the numerous inscriptions lining the funerary chapel of Cardinal Giacomo of Portugal (d. 1459), designed and executed in San Miniato between 1460 and 1466 by Antonio and Bernardo Rossellino. In this case, however, it is set where it hardly can be read. Carved on the lower curve of the sarcophagus, it brings to mind certain baroque inventions of partial legibility that were still far in the future.

Luca della Robbia found a different solution to the central exhibition of funerary writing in the funerary monument of Benozzo Federighi, bishop of Fiesole (d. 1450), erected between 1454 and 1457 in San Miniato, in Florence. The inscription is in pure "Florentine" Romanesque capitals, set within a laurel crown supported by two angels, similar in design to the inscribed tondo at the beginning and end of various Florentine Humanist codices of the period. Two further splendid examples of the "Florentine manner" in the arrangement of funerary writing are the tomb of Barbara Manfredi (d. 1466), done by Francesco di Simone Ferrucci in San Mercuriale in Forlí, where the inscription, carved in Romanesque capitals, is arranged on a scroll partly unrolled by two putti, and the tomb of Medea Colleoni (d. 1470), executed by Giovanni Antonio Amadeo and now in the Colleoni Chapel in the cathedral of Bergamo, where the long inscription is innovatively laid out on a scroll, not below, but above the recumbent figure, a position still more centrally prominent in the architectonic complex.

3.   The two characteristic features of the "Florentine manner" of written death were the Romanesque-type capital and the undulating or

half-rolled scroll supported by two putti on which the inscription was engraved. Their disappearance marked the advent in Italy of a new way of conceiving the presence of writing on the tomb and of celebrating the dead by means of an inscribed text. The origin of this radical change was an upheaval in graphic taste brought about by the efforts of certain antiquarians and artists working in Padua, among them Felice Feliciano and Andrea Mantegna, who turned from Romanesque to classical models in their creation of ceremonial writing. This brought about a rebirth in the use of the capital of true classical type, for both epigraphy and the book, which rapidly established itself in the larger Italian centers during the seventies and eighties of the century.

The transfer of this new graphic typology into burial practice prompted a further heightening of the function of writing, a drastic reduction in the figurative element, and the paring down of the verbal message to short, classicizing formulations. It is no coincidence that in his *De re aedificatoria*, Alberti openly deprecates the "excessive prolixity" of contemporary epitaphs. In Florence, the first to experiment with the new, austerely sober, and emphatically graphic funerary language was Verrocchio, in the famous double tomb of Piero and Giovanni de' Medici in San Lorenzo, constructed between 1470 and 1472. The writing is set in two small tondi on a porphyry sarcophagus enclosed by an arch and confined by a bronze grille that serves as backdrop. The four sides of the base are also engraved in spacious capitals "all'antica."

But the main center of the new epigraphy was Rome, the great Rome of Sixtus IV, the Rome of Andrea Bregno and his workshop, of Bartolomeo Sanvito and his scripts, the former a sculptor, the latter a supreme calligrapher.

Immediately before and during the reign of Sixtus, Bregno and his collaborators proposed and imposed a model for the expression of written death that transformed the wall monument of medieval and Humanist-Florentine tradition into something profoundly different, an architectural, sculptural, and graphic complex in which each element, taken singularly, had an antique origin and stylization, while as a unit it constituted a substantially new complex. In its refined use of vegetation motifs, careful highlighting of antique references, and ample and extremely formal use of script of a classical epigraphic type, even if with manneristic modulations (the long palm-like *Y*, the extended tail of the *Q*), this strongly resembled the opening pages of the rich codices then being produced in Rome for the libraries of the pope and cardinals by highly skilled copyists and illuminators. Among the more out-standing craftsmen in the book field was the Venetian, Bartolomeo Sanvito, a graphic artist of genius, who exerted an undoubted influ-ence on the establishment and canonization in the seventies of the epi-graphic capital known, after the reigning pope, as "Sistine." But since the first Roman monument in the new "antiquarian" style, with the new epigraphic script, is actually that erected by Bregno in Santa Maria in Aracoeli to Cardinal Ludovico d'Albret, who died in 1465, the first appearance of this new graphic stylization seems to have occurred ear-lier, even if not much earlier, than the papacy of Sixtus IV, and, proba-bly, the presence and work of Sanvito in Rome. The examples of "Sis-tine" funerary epigraphy created in Rome between the early seventies and the end of the fifteenth century are very numerous indeed and cannot all be mentioned here, though they well deserve to be for the quality of their execution. As examples, let me just cite the funerary monument to Pietro Riario (d. 1474) in Santi Apostoli, which has script in two different sizes precisely laid out on an enormous plaque; that of Iacopo Alberini (d. 1476) in Santa Maria sopra Minerva on an ancient reused sarcophagus; that of Giovanni della Rovere (d. 1483) in Santa Maria del Popolo, where the inscription occupies an imposing position on a large tabella ansata (an ancient motif); that of Marco Antonio Albertoni (d. 1485), in the same church, where the inscription occupies an enormous surface covering the whole sarcophagus and constitutes the most important and visible spatial element in the whole monument.

In its return to classicizing models, Sistine funerary epigraphy did not merely take up the scheme of inscription on a large plaque or tabella ansata but went through significant variations. Some monu-ments, like that in Santa Maria sopra Minerva of Dietisalvi Nerone (d. 1482)—a Florentine, and it can hardly be a coincidence that, in Flo-rentine fashion, a scroll appears on it—have several writing spaces, har-monizing and contrasting at the same time. Other monuments from close to the end of the century show a return to the entirely classical motif of two relief busts in flanking niches. One at least—that in Santa Maria Maggiore dedicated to his brother Stefano—is the work of the great Humanist Bartolomeo Platina. It consists of a simple, extremely classical slab with three superimposed strips carved with a refined bilin-gual Greek and Latin text of utmost purity of letter design and layout. After the death of Sixtus, it fell to Antonio del Pollaiolo, a Florentine artist working in Rome, to design and build the dead pope's monument. He worked on it between 1484 and 1493 and for it chose—or was forced to choose, in line with the dead pope's wish—the medieval model of the slab with recumbent figure taken up by Donatello many decades earlier. The result is a further heightening of the role of epigraphical writing in the classical style. It is laid out on a large plaque at the foot of the deceased and spreads over books held open by the Virtues in the lateral friezes.

From Rome to Florence: toward the end of the century in the Sassetti Chapel in Santa Trinita—constructed by wish of Francesco Sassetti, the merchant-Humanist friend of Lorenzo de' Medici—an artist, perhaps Giuliano da Sangallo, taking up a motif of Verrocchio's, placed a sarcophagus under a niche. A sober inscription of classical formula stands out on it in solitary splendor. Behind the altar of the same chapel, Domenico Ghirlandaio painted a fresco of the Nativity and included an ancient sarcophagus with a long, allusive inscription.

References, reshaping, quotations: the whole of fifteenth-century Italian funerary art, given a new rhetoric of words, forms, and script by the humanists and by archaizing artists, is marked by a continuous play of revival, of harking back, of return to the past, created by and for a group of people who were at once an aware and cultivated public and refined participants. These in their turn saw themselves as performing the social task of public celebration for an increasingly restricted elite of government, power, and money consisting of churchmen and laity, of great lords, merchants, and military adventurers, to whom the new mode of death written "all'antica" was very welcome as conceptual consecration and social identification of their good fortune on earth.

From the Stone to the Page

1. "What has so far hardly come to the fore—the difference in the expression of the sense of death between Italy and the Franco-Germanic area—from now on looms very large. There was not only a disparity of forms, but indeed, a total lack of parallelism between the two areas." So said Alberto Tenenti in a famous book published in 1957. The differences in expression that he pointed out in the theme of death during the Renaissance period reappear with equal force and clarity when one looks at the graphic aspects of funerary production. Clearly, this was not just a matter of the survival of the figurative motif of the *transi*, the decaying corpse, that continued to be reproduced, at least in France, practically down to the threshold of the Enlightenment. It was, rather, the survival of medieval forms of funerary writing, the strip on tombstone or monument, the use of Gothic script, minuscule or capital, but especially, the rejection of a central and unitary placing for funerary writing that, with the return to classical layout, had been the great rediscovery of the Italian Renaissance.

    In France and in Germany (but even in Spain), there was continued use into the fifteenth and sixteenth centuries and beyond both of stone or metal pavement slabs (though absolute primacy in quality and number goes undoubtedly to England) and of monuments raised in some way above the ground, with a recumbent effigy of the deceased (or deceased couple) and the writing set either on the border or on a plaque at the foot of the figure. The general European use of the wall monument also continued, especially in the case of great prelates, and the perhaps rarer one of the simple inscribed slab.

    In particular, *transi* tombs, with representations of the dead body in decay, continued to have plural inscriptions, moral and edifying maxims, and scriptural passages scattered in various positions over the funerary monument, addressed to their readers as illustration and comment on the lugubrious display. These constitute a veritable funerary microliterature intended to give information, making wide use of the vulgar tongue and necessarily employing a Gothic minuscule and strip or double column layout for maximum compression of the writing in the restricted spaces available for exhibition.

Thus, the tombstone of Jean Fievez (d. 1425), now in the Brussels Museum, which shows him dead in bed surrounded by his brethren, has writing (in French, not Latin) scattered practically all over: in three lines set on the lower edge, in a "strip cartoon" scroll above the dead man's head, in yet another scroll, and on the pages of an open book. The great tomb of Archbishop Henry Chichele (d. 1443) in Canterbury cathedral shows the deceased recumbent in prayer and, lower down, in decay, while the written text is split between a traditional epigraph set above and two moralizing inscriptions set next to the *transi*. Again, in the complex tomb of Canon Etienne Yver (d. 1467) in Notre-Dame in Paris, the writing is scattered over five different areas, including a book, scrolls, and the edge of the sarcophagus.

In contrast to the classicizing style of fifteenth-century Italy, a central feature of funerary writing in the north (but also in Spain) is its abundance of epigraphical text, no matter the language of expression (Latin or the local tongue) or the form of layout. Practically the whole space available on the Paris tombstone of the alchemist Nicholas Flamel (d. 1418), erected while he was alive, is occupied—apart from a strip above with the representation of three saints and one below for that of the *transi* corpse—by three dense vernacular texts in Gothic minuscule, laid out in eleven lines at the center of the slab, on a scroll next to the corpse and in a proper inscription of three lines on the lower edge. One could easily multiply examples.

All this suggests a profound tendency in the process of representation and control of death that entailed a desire to express and communicate. Indeed, these tombs had a specifically informative function. The devout public found itself addressed by a long discourse, variously structured in images and texts, set up on every funerary monument. The macabre dwelling on death intrinsic to *transi* portrayal—restricted, in only seeming contradiction, to figures of great importance in the lay and ecclesiastical hierarchies—had of necessity to be repeated and explained to the public of the faithful by suitable written comment that would incite them to meditation, participation, and awe. And this in its turn was an instrument of a northern religiosity that made a daily practice of reading liturgical, scriptural, and edifying texts in the vernacular, very much more so than its Italian counterpart.

2.   "Fame keeps epitaphs lying quiet; it goes not forward or backward because they are dead, and their doing is done." This startling and enigmatic thought, an idea perhaps for a sonnet, was set down without correction or second thoughts by Michelangelo in the lower margin of a sketch for the monumental tomb (never built) of the so-called "Magnifici" (Lorenzo and Giuliano de' Medici *seniores*) intended for the Medici Chapel in San Lorenzo in Florence. It was there, from 1520–21 onward, as we know, that amid crises, interruptions, and difficulties of every sort, he engaged in a great work of creation. The jotting clearly relates to the designing of the Medici tombs on which, though there are spaces set aside for epigraphical writing, there are no "epitaphs." This is in line with the well-known rejection of exhibited writing to which Michelangelo, a specialist in the "unwritten" as well as the "unfinished," remained faithful, except on extremely rare occasions. But what exactly did he mean by the phrase? First of all, perhaps, he is referring to the necessary and binding relationship between fame and funerary inscription, and then the unchangeable fixity in the situation of the dead, whose "doing is done," halted by death. If the interpretation does not seem too far-fetched, one might suggest that his point is the supreme futility of the genre of writing represented by "epitaphs," which, in their motionless "lying quiet," can only express a situation dictated and determined by "fame," immutable, and thus removed from truth and life. Hence his rejection of the practice, and the absence of exhibited writing, replaced by plaques that, though highlighted by emphatic framing, remain empty. The rejection probably also derived from a cognate distrust of the rhetorical and entirely Latin culture of the composers of the increasingly rich texts of contemporary funerary epigraphy. Michelangelo had learned to write in "mercantile" cursive and remained faithful to the vernacular throughout his long life; his relationship with writing could hardly not have been Tuscan and "bourgeois."

All this seems confirmed by another episode relating to funerary practices and occasioned by the death in Rome, on January 8, 1544, of

Cecchino Bracci, the fifteen-year-old nephew of Luigi Del Riccio, a very dear friend and colleague of Michelangelo's. Del Riccio's persistence resulted in a promise to design "an honest tomb" for the boy, and Michelangelo did in fact make a sketch. This was later used by Pietro Urbano for the memorial in Santa Maria in Aracoeli, in Rome, though he changed its proportions and inserted an inscription on either side of the portrait. But Michelangelo's concern to celebrate the dead youth did not end there. Del Riccio asked him, and other literary friends such as Donato Giannotti and Carlo Gondi (the author of an epigram inscribed in the epigraph on the right of the tomb), to compose verse epitaphs. Michelangelo initially committed himself to writing fifteen, as recorded in a half-serious letter addressed to his insistent friend: "Now the promise of fifteen vouchers is fulfilled; I am no longer bound by it." But then, solicited by pleas and gifts and gripped by the literary challenge, he went on to compose as many as fifty.

They consist of sonnets or quatrains in which all possible aspects of the relationship between life and death, youth, the human lot, and so on, are handled with a particular gusto for complex expression, while the text always retains the form of the epitaph proper, in which the dead boy sometimes speaks in the first person ("Here am I dead believed"; "Here am I buried"), and sometimes the tomb itself ("Here I clasp the Braccio" [a pun on "braccio," "arm," and the boy's surname]; "Of Cechin am I, that here lies dead"). Naturally, these were not epitaphs to be engraved on hard material, set on a tomb, and publicly exhibited, but a literary product that was part of a practice Michelangelo engaged in to the utmost, relishing in the best Florentine vernacular tradition a playful aspect he freely confessed to: "Clumsy things; but since it's wished I make a thousand there's no help but all kind of thing be in them." As paper epitaphs, written in verse and in the vulgar tongue, produced in large numbers in competition with himself and with his friends, part of a literary game that was rapidly becoming a fashion, they avoided being the kind of epitaph, solemnly composed and carved in Latin, kept "lying quiet" by Fame.

During the sixteenth century, there was a return, in Italy and elsewhere in Europe, from the terse neoclassical epigraphy of Italian humanism to the taste for the expanded epitaph on a large plaque, or even divided between two writing spaces on the tomb. It was, however, a phenomenon of wider proportions and brought about by deeper causes than mere taste. The fact was that the power and government elites, the sponsors of funerary writing everywhere in Europe, had begun to display a preference for individually particularized forms of memorial epigraphy of an almost documentary nature instead of the sober formulations "all'antica." The result of this change in taste and mentality was that within a few decades, the classicizing model, full of descriptive and narrative textuality, embodying several sections of dense script, changed into something profoundly different from the original fifteenth-century archetype.

Andrea Sansovino initiated the change at the start of the century with two imposing Roman tombs, that of Ascanio Maria Sforza (d. 1505) and that of Girolamo Basso Della Rovere (d. 1507), both erected in Santa Maria del Popolo in Rome and both ostentatious and grandiose. The sumptuous funerary monument to Cardinal Francesco Quiñones in Santa Croce in Gerusalemme, again in Rome, is also by Sansovino and has two inscribed plaques, one above, with a red background, the other set low . There is visible conflict in the classical funerary monument of Pietro Bembo, erected by Michele Sammicheli in Sant'Antonio in Padua, between the austere design with single epigraph and the diffuse, dense nature of the text laid out on a plaque below the deceased's bust, which states that the tomb was erected "lest posterity lose the memory of the body of a person whose intellectual creations are eternal." And the Camposanto in Pisa, once a communal burial ground, was being gradually transformed into a monumental sepulchral structure. The first element in this process was the wall monument to the jurist Giovanni Francesco Vegio (d. 1554), which has an inscribed plaque set below the sarcophagus.

But, as I said, this was a trend common to the century. Even outside Italy, the classicizing wall monument was being transformed into a massive, rich, ornamental construction with ample spaces devoted to writing. The tomb of Louis de Brézé (d. 1531) in Rouen cathedral follows the Italian model with a triumphal arch, but above the *transi* body two large plaques with dense, diffuse inscriptions, in French and deriving from a different graphic model, stand out with great boldness. It was Italian artists who brought to Spain the model of the wall tomb with imposing graphic inserts. Giovanni Merliano, for example, designed the tomb of Ramon Cardona, viceroy of Naples (d. 1522) in Bellpuig, in which a colossal plaque in large capitals in the classical style dominates the whole construction from the top of the triumphal arch, while Pompeo Leoni was responsible for the large tomb of Don

Ferdinando de Valdés (d. 1587) in the collegiate church of Salas, which has two imposing plaques in closely written capitals set into the arched structure.

The model caught on and spread to England, as well. A fine example is the tomb of the Earl of Rutland (d. 1591), executed in Bottesford (Leicestershire) by the Dutchman Garret Johnson, in which two flanking plaques dense with text stand out above the recumbent bodies of the married couple. A little later, at the start of the new century, the funerary monument of Queen Elizabeth I (d. 1603) in Westminster Abbey, in the shape of a small temple, has long inscriptions with gilded letters and perfect capitals in the Italian Renaissance style, carved on black slabs.

Everywhere, in short, the gigantism of the large mannerist tombs—increasingly decked with ornamentation, figures, drapery, columns, and arches—went along with a great profusion of writing, often gilded or in metal, and of corresponding texts. Everywhere, especially in the gloomy atmosphere of the first half of that great century, funerary epigraphy and its cultivated authors celebrated the splendors of an aristocracy of the Church (or Churches), of arms, and of power that was eager to proclaim itself and tell its tale, to portray itself and set down expansively in writing its merits and titles, the extent and solidity of its good fortune. This on the point of death, and even beyond it.

3.   Soon, the necessarily limited epigraphical text no longer seemed adequate to represent the written memory of the illustrious dead. Apart from anything else, it was stationary, bound by its material link with the tomb, by its enforced solidarity with the corpse. A society of widespread literacy needed texts, even of a funerary kind, that could circulate, be read, recited, quoted, exchanged, and reproduced. The text was thus freed from the immobile singularity of the epigraph and entrusted to the mobile reproducibility of the book. New written funerary products, more properly and directly literary in character and made of paper, made their appearance alongside the true epigraphical text.

The verse compositions begged from Michelangelo by a persistent friend have already been mentioned, but the phenomenon itself was much older and dates back to the final years of the fifteenth century, to the last and refined representatives of Neapolitan humanism, who gathered round the moribund Aragonese dynasty. Their greatest spokesman was Giovanni Gioviano Pontano, an accomplished humanist and a fine Latin poet. Imbued with a sense of the pathos of death and endowed with a natural bent for the funerary lament, he found outlet for his particular sensibility in two ways. First, through the erection in his adopted city of Naples of a funerary shrine on which, and in which, he set up a series of commemorative epigraphs for his wife Adriana, who died in 1490, for their children who had died young, and for himself, along with other epigraphs from the classical period. He also composed a variety of epitaphs for friends and acquaintances, the famous and the less so. These were destined to become part of his poetic works, the two books of the *Tumuli* that he polished until the end of his life and that were published posthumously in 1505 in the edition by Summonte.

The *Tumuli* constitutes the very first modern literary collection of epitaphs in verse, and they hark back to a poetic tradition of the classical age, in particular, to the funerary odes in the *Anthologia Palatina*, the *Planudea* version of which was printed for the first time in Florence in 1494. Pontano did not deny his borrowing from the past; indeed, he highlights it in an elegant play of reference and quotation, but the elements of invention and novelty prevail over the rich patrimony of tradition. The majority of his 113 compositions are formally presented as epitaphs, but in reality they were not, in the sense that they were almost never carved and exhibited. (Some of them are very long.) And yet very often, if not always, the situations are those proper to ancient funerary epigraphs: dialogues between the passerby and the dead, or his "genius," or his "umbra"; addresses by the dead, by the passerby, by the poet, by the "tumulus" itself; laments from relatives, lovers, or the dead person himself; and elegy and eulogy, usually by the poet in the first person. But the presence of particular cases, such as that of a young woman slain for adultery (2, 12) or playful compositions on the death of animals or particular people, reveal the true nature of the collection. It is a purely literary production, characterized by a high degree of whimsical pathos unsuited to embodiment in stone and requiring the textual effusion and diffusion ensured by its book format.

The genre went on to success. Pontano's collection—odes by a single author for various of the dead—was followed by other collections of funerary odes by many authors in honor of a single dead person. Apart from a short precedent, a handful of odes published in about

1477 in memory of the young Alessandro Cinuzzi, who died at sixteen and who had been close to Girolamo Riario, nephew of Sixtus IV, the first of these was published in Bologna in 1504 by Caligola Bazalieri. Modestly printed, the *Collettanee greco-latine e vulgari per diversi auctori moderni nella morte dell'ardente Seraphino Aquilano* contained odes collected and arranged by Giovanni Filoteo Achillini, a minor man of letters from a Bolognese family known to the history of poetry for other reasons. The "funerary procession," the "small compendium of fragments in miscellany or collection" put together by Achillini, includes few texts that propose themselves as epitaphs proper. The features of the genre had already been defined, and they are those of the elegy, of the recollection, of the "poem in honor of," and any relationship with the purpose of the epigraph and its place on the tomb seems to have all but disappeared.

4.   The collecting of epigraphs could mean many different things in the cultivated Italy of the early sixteenth century, and before the Sack of 1527, it took various forms in Rome. The outstanding example is the famous large anthology of antique epigraphs (many of them funerary) published by Giacomo Mazzocchi in 1521 under the title *Epigrammata antiquae urbis*. And it was certainly no accident that in 1519, the same publisher published a collection of 37 odes in memory of Celso Archelao Melini, nephew of Pope Innocent VIII, and in 1522 another analogous collection for the death of Marco Antonio Colonna. Both were entitled *Lachrimae* and introduced a strong dose of pathos that was to have success for centuries.

Mazzocchi's activity over a span of barely four years brings out another aspect of funerary literature on paper, then beginning to stand alongside stone. This lies in the relationship—of emulation, of imitation, of study half antiquarian and half literary—with the ancient heritage common to humanists and poets, serious seekers after truth and fatuous courtiers. All were fond of blurring differences between the two levels, passing from a lament for a dead friend to the transcription of an ancient epitaph, and vice versa.

The cultural climate was such that despite their material fragility, paper and book poetry seemed to have given the literati greater guarantee of endurance over time than that offered by the seemingly more solid epigraphical production:

For if time breaks the statues and the stones
and the glory of the tombs is unsure and brief
solely in song might I soar in flight.

So Sannazaro declares in his *Rime* of 1530, pointing to the way "fame" was becoming literalized and involved with the book, no longer finding its highest expression in funerary epigraph, as it had for centuries, but in the "song," in poetry written in Latin and Greek, or in any of the national languages for that matter. Later, in a 1574 work devoted to the *Funerali antichi di diversi popoli et nationi,* Tommaso Porcacchi registered the established status of the new literary genre: "today, we are accustomed to write verses in every language in honor of the dead." He follows this declaration with a list of collections by various hands recently published in Italy. Among them was a volume, famous in its time, published in Venice in 1561 in honor of Irene di Spilimbergo, who had died at barely eighteen years old, sung in Latin, but mostly in Italian, by many poets: the young Tasso, Laura Terracina, Luigi Tansillo, Luca Contile, and various others.

The phenomenon was European in scale. In France, Jean Dorat, the poet royal and member of the Collège de France, wrote a poem for the death of the Connétable Anne de Montmorency (d. 1567), entitled *Sur le tombeau de messire Anne de Mommorency*, in which the locative indicates not an actual fact, but one of occasion. The poem was *for* the tomb in fact, that is, for the death of Anne Montmorency, but not meant to be set and exhibited *on* the tomb itself. Many other examples, long and short, appeared in the rich collection of *Epitaphes* by his best-known disciple, Pierre de Ronsard, who raised the genre to a high degree of literary refinement while respecting its conventions and formal canons. In this altogether literary phenomenology of funerary writing, it was no longer a matter of writing the dead, but of writing of the dead, or better, *about* the dead.

Those purely literary episodes of collection, of anthologization, of the spread of books of epigraphical texts clearly aimed at satisfying the tastes of a public increasingly interested in the genre and ever more eager to read examples, were also of this kind. Throughout the sixteenth century, Italy, and particularly the capital cities, such as Venice and Rome, remained the area of Europe that produced the highest number of inscriptions, funerary and otherwise, and that held the primacy and dictated the rules of the modern epigraphical style to other countries, which looked to it for inspiration and models.

Early in the second half of the century, Lorenz Schrader, a young and cultivated German from Halberstadt, came to Italy to study and spent three years visiting its larger and smaller cities. Struck by the excellence and number of modern epigraphs, and especially by funerary inscriptions in churches and on monuments, he began transcribing them, enriching his collection during a later journey in 1567, and later again with the help of an anonymous assistant. Undoubtedly on the advice of some of the greatest German scholars of the time—Melanchthon (who died in 1560), Joachim Camerarius, Johannes Sturm, and Georg Fabricius—he reedited his collection and published it in 1592 under the title *Monumentorum Italiae quae hoc nostro saeculo et a Christianis posita sunt libri quatuor*, openly acknowledging Italian primacy in the epigraphic and funerary sphere. "One must in fact admit that in composing and setting up epitaphs and inscriptions, the Italians by far surpass other nations" (108v). Schrader's large volume had no illustrations, and the author himself regrets the fact. But modern epigraphy, and funerary epigraphy in particular, must already have been in fashion if by 1574 another German, Siegfried Rybisch, could persuade Tobias Fendt, an engraver from Bratislava, to publish a collection of prints illustrating more than one hundred and fifty funerary monuments, ancient and modern, from every part of Europe (the majority Italian), under the title *Monumenta sepulcrorum cum epigraphis ingenio et doctrina excellentium virorum aliorum tam prisci quam nostri saeculi memorabilium hominum de archetypis expressa*. It was a purely illustrative collection of prints, practically devoid of text, with mediocre reproductions of inscriptions and monuments, the main interest of which was not so much antiquarian as literary and artistic. Fortune smiled on it and—in contrast to Schrader's ampler and better-documented work—it was a remarkable success, as evinced by the numerous editions published up to 1671.

These sparse but significant examples are intended to show how death—written wherever and in whatever way—turned into a literary product of general interest during the first half of the sixteenth century in Europe. The aristocratic and governing elites and the high urban bourgeoisie identified with the values it represented for reasons of prestige, while the intellectuals and an ever more widespread and increasingly compact, cultivated public did so for literary reasons and as a matter of taste. Those who possessed even the lowest title or rank preferred to be buried in churches or their immediate neighborhood.

This meant that sacred edifices were occupied for funerary purposes and inevitably turned into lavish and crowded cemeteries, in the form of both permanent monuments and temporary burials that took over the remaining space. The scale of the phenomenon must have been very considerable if Pope Pius V, a stern interpreter of the spirit of Trent, had to emit a bull ("Cum primum," of April 1, 1566) on the observance of worship in churches in which he explicitly orders rectors to remove the deposits of the dead "existing above ground" and bury the "bodies of the dead in deep tombs in the ground." Thus, the dead body was committed to the earth, while pomp and writing—as message, witness, and guarantee of the living to the living—were left to stand on the surface.

The Theaters of Pain

1.   "Roman antiquity . . . not yet having either taste or knowledge of the human arts, composed its inscriptions with a terse gravity, but without any liveliness or point at all." Thus, in one stroke, *Il cannocchiale aristotelico* (first edition, Turin, 1655), a celebrated book by the Jesuit Emanuele Tesauro that tells us a great deal about the seventeenth-century cultural climate, wipes out the great classical epigraphical tradition on which the whole of cultured Europe had relied, or at least had claimed to rely, from the fifteenth century on. This rejection did not occur merely on the level of literary style, of pure and simple rhetoric, or of the entirely new taste for the conceit, for wit, for the seeking after verbal marvels. It manifested itself also, if not especially, on the material level of monument building. From the end of the sixteenth century and particularly from the early years of the seventeenth century onward, in Italy and then gradually in France and elsewhere, epigraphy had a new ordinance, occupied new spaces, and expressed itself in forms different from those of the ancient past and even from those of the period just gone by.

Not only funerary epigraphy—which held on to its numerical and qualitative primacy even during the seventeenth and eighteenth centuries—but the whole of Baroque epigraphy is marked by highly visible innovations in placing and aspect. Most noticeable, perhaps, are the carving of writing on stone that mimicked such pretendedly unsuitable materials as drapery, ribbons, and scrolls; the layout in curving lines; the multicolored backgrounds and letters; and the use of formats absolutely unknown to previous tradition.

In the Baroque cities of Italy and Europe, all this was accentuated by the multiplication of funerary monuments in churches and an awareness of the constant presence of death in the daily life of the city, especially in the great and monumental cities where a sizable aristocracy, representatives of the high clergy, and the great bourgeoisie all were concerned to celebrate and record their dead in a continual repetition of writing in ephemeral form, in mobile form (books, pamphlets, handbills), as well as in the stable form of tombs. All this was the product of a common and widespread culture in which—especially in its more properly religious aspects—death and the dead were very much present, aroused great interest, and constituted a consciously felt relationship of continuity and closeness with the living.

There is a great deal of well-attested evidence for this mental attitude, including wills, painting and sculpture, literature and sermons, and the cult of saints, martyrs, and relics. Into this current flowed a certain taste for the morbid, pleasure in visual spectacle, and an ostentatious pathos, all profoundly felt and enjoyed by a participant public. This strong interest—cloaked always by devotion—in the subject of death could easily slip into exasperated forms of publicly displayed asceticism and a direct and pronounced interest in the dead and in corpses as such. Though anatomy had become a scientific study, certain keenly observed illustrations betray a frisson of indulgence and more than a hint of maniacal obsession. Take, for example, the treatise *Anatomia per uso et intelligenza del disegno* by Bernardino Genga, published in Rome in 1691, in which one of the opening plates (no. 2) centers on a loculus opened by a winged Death and two conversing skeletons to reveal a heap of tangled skeletons. Or consider the cemeteries of the Capuchins, with their rows of corpses decked out as a spine-chilling spectacle for public consumption. It was, as I said, a question of themes, attitudes, and practices everywhere present and symptomatic of a climate, a taste, the fashion of a world that relished the joys of life as profoundly as it was fond of puzzling rhetorically over the mystery of death and the decay of the flesh "into earth, into soil, into dust, into shade, into nothing"—as Luis de Góngora put it.

2.   This interest in dead bodies also meant a concern for tombs and funerals, both past and present. A cultural attitude already present in sixteenth-century Europe, generated out of literary curiosity and antiquarian interest, had spread by the mid-seventeenth century to take on the modalities and aspect of a shared pattern of behavior that fixed

models for a practice—that of written death—increasingly generalized and valued. How else to explain the immense collection of drawings—accurate even down to the inscriptions—in the Gaignères collection? It certainly explains works like the corpus put together
though the lengthy efforts of John Weever—impressive aside from its
sparse, crude, woodcut illustration—of a large number of *Ancient Funerall Monuments Within the United Monarchie of Great Britain, Ire-
land, and the Islands Adiacent . . .* , published in London in 1631,
which, despite its title, covers only the four dioceses of Canterbury,
Rochester, London, and Norwich. On quite another level, it explains
the *Epigraphae religiosae, memoriales, mortuales, encomiasticae,* a collection of funerary epigraphs published in Rome in 1670 by the Barn-
abite man of letters Ottavio Boldoni, and the *Inscriptiones* by
Emanuele Tesauro, the Jesuit already mentioned, edited by Emanuele
Filiberto Panebianco and published in several editions from 1666 onward. It also explains the *Theatrum funebre* and the *Hortus variarum
inscriptionum,* published in Salzburg by Otto Aicher in 1673–75 and
1676, respectively.

The epigraphical texts these books strove to collect and publish became increasingly numerous, displaced, scattered, separated, and mar-
ginalized on the surface of the seventeenth-century funerary monuments, as in the spaces offered by that ephemeral and imposing antici-
pation, the public funeral ceremony. Exhibited funerary writing in
Baroque Europe—as compared with the Renaissance adoption of classical usage—lost its centrality, renounced in favor of various place-
ments and arrangements on the body of the monuments or tableaux.
But the main development lay in the increasing frequency of texts,
long and short, scattered everywhere in mottoes, scriptural quotations,
and phrases. This capricious and unstable presence of writing, often
on folded drapery, on curving surfaces, on rolled "cartouches," went
along with another tendency in contemporary taste, an indulgence in
pathos and the dramatic display of feelings that purely informative
texts needed to comment on and underline if they were to prompt distress and commiseration. According to an anonymous description of
the funeral ceremony held in the cathedral of Florence for the death
of Pope Leo XI (1605), "there was such a mixture of pity and awed respect in people's minds that they were in the mood to weep, giving
forth bitter tears and burning sighs with strong conviction."

3.   The novelties introduced during the sixteenth and seventeenth centuries into the European conception and embodiment of the written record of the illustrious dead centered not on the tomb, but on the funeral procession. Very often this took place far from the site of death, of the funeral, or even of the actual burial, a grandiose but ephemeral spectacle "in absentia" of the body. They are described in ever richer and more splendid detail in written (and illustrated) reports of the event that quote the displayed texts with maniacal completeness, if not philological precision. According to André Chastel, "one of the most typical remains of the period is perhaps those enormous portfolios in which the great funeral ceremonies are commemorated in prints." All seems to have begun with the memorial ceremony that took place in 1558 in various European cities to mourn the death of the Emperor Charles V (d. September 21, 1558), and in particular that in Piacenza on December 21 and the grandiose one that followed in Brussels on the twenty-eighth of the same month. The phenomenon developed in Florence, spreading thence to Rome and elsewhere. The funeral rites of Michelangelo Buonarroti, who had died in Rome on February 18, 1564, were solemnly celebrated "in absentia" in the church of San Lorenzo (Florence) on June 28 that year. The writings included a large epigraph composed by Pier Vettori, various pieces of biographical detail, and mottoes and poems in Latin and the vernacular by "certain fine wits," among them Benedetto Varchi, Angelo Bronzino, Laura Battiferro, and Giovanni Battista Adriani, all freely affixed "on the burial place." Ten years later, again in San Lorenzo, the "funeral ceremony" of Grand Duke Cosimo de' Medici was held; all of the 36 Latin inscriptions are given in the corresponding anonymous report.

Up to almost the end of the sixteenth century, the printed accounts recording and documenting the spectacle of the funeral ceremony and reproducing the displayed texts, were small-format pamphlets, generally without illustration, modeled on the genre and tradition of the *avviso*, the public notice. But as early as 1591, *La pompa funerale fatta dall'ill.mo et r.mo sr. Cardinale Montalto* [Alessandro Peretti] *nella trasportatione dell'ossa di papa Sisto il Quinto . . .* , published in Rome in 1591, contains a general view of the procession—including the structure designed by Domenico Fontana—engraved by Girolamo Rinaldi, as well as some handsome copperplate prints by Francesco Villamena showing the statue and its inscriptions. With the new century, reports became fuller, more sumptuous, larger in format, and more richly illustrated. Particularly splendid is Lelio Guidiccioni's *Breve racconto della trasportatione del corpo di papa Paolo IV dalla basilica di San Pietro a quella di S. Maria Maggiore . . .* , published in Rome in 1623 in folio, with eighteen large prints engraved by Theodor Crüger and an exact transcription of the many inscriptions, more densely concentrated on the catafalque, where four putti "opened and spread out very great cascades of cloth of gold and black on which four inscriptions could be read" (53). What was probably the largest number of funerary inscriptions dedicated to a single person appeared in Rome in 1627, not, surprisingly, to a great prelate or politician, but to Sitti Manni Gioerida, Persian wife of the traveler Pietro della Valle. Inscriptions in Latin, Chaldean, Italian, Arabic, Portuguese, Turkish, French, Persian, Spanish, Armenian, and modern and classical Greek were arranged around her catafalque in a quite extraordinary plethora of characters, along with a series of verse compositions "hung about the urn" by "gentlemen of the academy."

Writing performed an essential function in the spectacle of the funeral ceremony. "Inscriptions are the most essential part of funerary decorations because they are its soul. They illustrate the subjects, they give speech to the figures, the emblem, and the coats of arms," said Claude François Menestrier in a quite singular book on funeral decorations published in Paris in 1684 and still justly famous.

The number of written texts accompanying the funerary rite was very high, not least because the number of possibilities and surfaces suitable for writing was also very high. The writing was mainly set above and around the catafalque, which usually occupied the center of the church. Then, biographical information and mottoes were fixed on the tableaux and statues adorning the aisles. One or more inscriptions were set up on the back wall, and another, or others, on the facade. Finally, the verses composed spontaneously or on commission by men of letters, academics, and nobles were handed out on loose leaves, the texts of which were then usually published in an appendix to the printed report of the ceremony. Overall, there might be 30 to 60 or even more inscribed texts of differing nature and extent, all addressed to a public eager to see and read, to enjoy the texts (often in Latin and Italian) as they did the images and the tableaux.

In the first half of the eighteenth century, books recording grand funeral ceremonies became real masterpieces of the printer's and etcher's art, very large in format, rich in texts, vignettes, and ornamented initials, with large folding copper etchings done by the finest artists of the time. Once again, Rome offers examples of unusual richness. The first is the *Relacion de las exequias* of Philip V of Spain, published in 1746 with seven large prints executed by Giuseppe Vasi, Louis Le Lorrain, and others. A second is the *Funerali di Giacomo III re della Gran Brettagna . . .* , published in 1766 in a folio volume of great splendor and formal accuracy.

When Menestrier published his treatise in 1684, he was able to list as many as 116 reports of public and state funeral ceremonies and to suggest that at least five hundred such ceremonies must have taken place in the various cities of Europe over the preceding hundred years. The phenomenon was undoubtedly on a larger scale and profoundly marked the religious sentiments, the collective imagination, and the graphic culture of the urban populations of the larger European cities. Though exhibited funerary writing was one of the fundamental elements, it played only a subordinate, merely informative and decorative role compared with the ceremonial and the tableaux. This was a characteristic feature of the period, common, even if in lesser measure, to funerary monuments proper, as to all contemporary epigraphy.

4.   In the seventeenth and eighteenth centuries, the prevailing graphico-spatial models used in funerary epigraphy were those prompted by the widespread and impressive practice of the funeral ceremony. They betray an obsessive abuse and a fierce and continuous formal reshaping of writing. Even on the funerary monuments of the period writing was employed in texts that were sometimes spread everywhere. It was scattered over several areas of the writing space, sometimes even running over the bounding edge of the monument. It was given a nonlinear, curved, undulating, irregular layout, and took on vivid color against backgrounds themselves colored (gold on black, yellow on red). It was set on writing surfaces that feigned to be material other than the actual stone and marble they in fact were: velvet, cloth, hide, wood, parchment, or paper.

These phenomena were present everywhere to differing degrees and may therefore be considered European, at least at the highest levels of funerary memorial, where fashion, a shared artistic culture, and the influences of schools succeeded in imposing largely analogous structures and end products. Of necessity I can cite only a few examples that make for a clearer view of the general tendencies in the use of written memory and its relationship with other aspects of tomb monuments during the age we generically define as Baroque.

Transforming the material, forcing a smooth, hard, marble surface to imitate the wrinkles in cloth, then setting on it a text in a vexed form, were all feats of ability and wit that the artistic sensibility of the time perceived as so many challenges, particularly in the written celebration of the dead. Many of the greatest Baroque sculptors tackled it, sometimes with stunning results, though here I can give no more than some representative instances. For Italy it is enough to record a few examples from Rome and Venice, the two great capitals of artistic taste and superior letter design. The De Silva funerary monument in Sant'Isidoro in Rome, with its very fine inscribed black marble drapery, was completed by Bernini in 1663. The tomb of Monsignor Mariano Pietro Vecchiarello (d. 1667) in San Pietro in Vincoli has an inscribed marble cloth supported by two skeletons. In Venice, there is the grandiose wall structure built by Bartolomeo Longhena in the church of the Frari for Doge Giovanni Pesaro (d. 1659, but 1666), where two large inscriptions stand out on marble cloth, composed, like the smaller ones below, by Emanuele Tesauro. To that may be added the monument to Antonio Savorgnan (d. 1627) in the church of the Beata Vergine in Udine, where the writing is scattered over three different areas, the last a marble "cloth" rounding off the whole. In England, there is the splendid monument to Doctor Busby in Westminster Abbey, the work of Francis Bird, where a cloth with a very long inscription, laid out in two columns, is draped over an aedicula set behind the figure of the dead man. The Hapsburg tomb in the Capuchin crypt in Vienna has a phantasmagoric collection of bronze sarcophagi with inscriptions set everywhere, even, for example, on the simulated banners hanging from the trumpets of the angels. In Germany, where writing—often set in ovals and on curved surfaces—in majuscule, in round minuscule, and in Gothic, is always very much employed, there is the funerary monument to Christoph von Freiberg (d. 1690) in the cathedral of Augsburg that has a long inscription set low on a shroud partially wrapping a skeleton. And from the end of the period, we have the large funerary monument to Vice-Chancellor Johann Adam Kopp (d. 1748) in the Universitätskirche of Marburg, where an inscription of 33 packed lines is carved on a long, rumpled cloth.

Gian Lorenzo Bernini was one of the great manipulators of materials in tomb sculpture and exhibited writing, his unique solutions always including the symbol of death. One should at least mention the tomb of Urban VIII (begun in 1628) in Saint Peter's, where a winged Death is caught in the act of writing the name of the dead pope on a large scroll. As the hand sets down the name, the gesture also conceals it, symbolically intimating an attempt at canceling written memory and prompting the reader to interpret and fill it out. Very probably the funerary monument to Doctor Valtrino in San Lorenzo in Damaso, where a winged Death supports a black cloth with writing, is also the work of Bernini.

The scattering of memorial writing over the monumental complex of the tomb is another of the structural features of written death in the Baroque period. It serves a double function, that of not disturbing the autonomy of the complex of images—by then often consisting of scenes of vivid drama—and that of allowing the written text to be distributed over several sections, exactly as in the ephemeral structures, with a main text and other complementary texts containing quotations, comment, and mottoes. Three of the most notable examples—none of them Italian and all the work of illustrious artists—are the celebrated tomb of Richelieu by François Girardon in the church of the Sorbonne in Paris, where the inscription is entirely separated from the theatrical, but peaceful scene of the cardinal's death (d. 1642); the funerary monument, now in the chapel of the Chateau de Chantilly, encasing the heart of Henry II Condé (d. 1646), the last work of Jacques Sarrazin, where the epigraphical text is inscribed on a side tablet held by one of the two genies portrayed; and finally, the funerary wall monument to Viscount Mordaunt erected in Fulham by John Bushnell, where the two inscriptions are set in oval discs beside the standing figure of the deceased.

Baroque epigraphy, as already suggested, was textually generous and diffuse. Funerary epigraphy was even more so, given that it had to provide documentary information, glorify the dead in its portrayal of careers and personalities, and flatter power while embracing it within the logic of devotion. This created a problem of space, accentuated by the marginalization and splitting of the writing, that was seen as a restricting factor by the more rhetorically skilled writers of epitaphs. In his already mentioned *Epigraphae*, Ottavio Boldoni records with regret how his epitaph for the tomb of Giuliano de' Medici, archbishop of Pisa, dated 1660, was badly carved for want of writing space, and the epigraph on the monument on the back wall of the Pisa cathedral remains marred by an excessive number of abbreviations and overcrowded lines. In those same years, Fabio Chigi, later Pope Alexander VII, was giving free rein to his epigraphical passion. As revealed in his commonplace books (for example Vatican Library ms, Chigi J. VI 205, cc. 299–303, 307–8), he, too, found himself subject to the recurrent blackmail of space. He was forced to make many drafts of inscriptions incorporating numerous corrections, counting the letters in each line, telling himself: "If it be necessary to abbreviate, one might reduce some word in the longer verses."

As must be evident, I have so far dealt only with learned creations, the ephemeral tableau or stable monument that everywhere consecrated the written memory of the more illustrious dead and celebrated their glory—along with that of the living who continued to administer their power and had commissioned their memorial. However, this was not the sole or definitive model for all the social categories in modern Europe that gradually were gaining the right to funerary writing, nor was it for every part of Europe, or for all funerary occasions. In northern and Protestant Europe especially, in Germany, the Scandinavian countries, in England and its American colonies, the so-called Baroque age was also (if not mainly) characterized by a throng of simple stones inscribed to the less famous dead in outdoor cemeteries close to churches, large and small. This, the alternative and very ancient model of funerary memory, was to persist for centuries in the daily life of millions of people and remains substantially unchanged in contemporary mass practices of written death.

Anglo-Americana

1. In 1631, John Weever, already mentioned as author of the first great anthology of English epitaphs, set down an ideal social hierarchy of written death in his preface on funerary monuments. He claims that the "person of . . . plebeian sort" should be buried without tomb, or stone, or epitaph of any kind; that middling landowners might have a stone, but no more; that the gentry of higher rank could have their effigies sculpted on a pedestal, but without arms; and that only nobles, princes, and kings had the right to a monumental tomb with a statue, alabaster, rich marble, and epitaphs exalting valor and virtue. Weever ends by complaining that of late, epitaphs were being given even to rich merchants and moneylenders.

In the first decades of the seventeenth century, in fact, a boom took place in Great Britain in the production of gravestones with decoration and texts in the vernacular for the middle and lower middle class: craftsmen, shop owners, and schoolteachers. This was obviously the result of a host of concomitant factors: the acquisition of reading and writing by a large part of the English population; the long struggle against the monarchy, waged by the middle classes and the lesser nobility, which led to the Civil War, the beheading of Charles I (1649), and Cromwell's Commonwealth; the enormous spread, at all levels of the population, of printed matter and books of a religious and political nature written in the vernacular; and Protestant religious feeling based on a personal reading of the Bible—to cite merely the most obvious. It is calculated that there are about five million tombstones in English graveyards, not counting those in churches. Though they mostly date from the eighteenth and nineteenth centuries, the impulse that led to such boundless use of inscribed memory came into being just as Weever was lamenting its first signs.

What were the main features of the funerary memorials that filled the typical graveyard of an English town or village? They were upright gravestones, curved or trilobate at the top, and usually carved with symbols or decoration. The writing space—the gravestone itself—was vast, sometimes bordered by figurative elements (angels, columns) that served to set it off. The texts, all in the vernacular, were generally lengthy and diffuse, beginning with the customary formula "Here lies" and followed by the particulars of the person, or persons, in the case of shared graves. The text almost always concluded with considerations of a religious nature, biblical quotations or short verse compositions. In some cases, there were also such short Latin formulas as "Memento mori" or similar expressions.

For its graphic style, the seventeenth century employed a rough capital, generally crudely carved and badly aligned, but based on models of "noble" epigraphy. The Gothic minuscule is rarely found. The early eighteenth century saw the advent of the round minuscule, which then established itself as the script most widely employed. By 1730, cursive had appeared, and its use became more frequent from 1780 onward, as variously shaped writing spaces, the cross shape, for example, were gradually adopted. The imagery was generally restricted to heads of cherubs, angels, and symbols of death, but sometimes real scenes were carved that structured and split the writing spaces. With the end of the eighteenth century, the traditional repertoire was enlivened by the introduction of typically neoclassical motifs.

Up to the mid-nineteenth century, the result was stable in its reiteration of traditional textual and formal models, while extremely various and original in its blending of motifs, newly devised layouts, and imagery. The various combinations of minuscule and majuscule, for example, that appeared during the eighteenth century are very singular.

2.   The Pilgrim fathers, and those who followed them across the ocean during the seventeenth century, took their customs, their English modes of thought and behavior, to the distant lands of the American colonies. The first settlers were highly literate, both because they came from a country where literacy was in any case widespread and

because almost all of them were deeply religious and accustomed to the daily perusal of Holy Scripture. But they did not merely know how to read, they knew how to write as well. In what soon became a highly urbanized and commercial microsociety where books and newspapers were common goods, almost all the settlers knew how to write, and wished and had to do so.

It is calculated that literacy among New England males in 1710 was around 70 percent, rising to 85 percent by 1760, and was very likely around 90 percent toward the end of the century. By the mid-seventeenth century, three-quarters of the male population of Boston were already literate, with few differences throughout the colonies and all social classes were involved. Given the strong Protestant conviction of the settlers and the animating presence of several urban centers, the problem of written death immediately arose and led to the establishment of a large number of graveyards very similar to their contemporary English counterparts and located, like them, close to churches.

But who in the American colonies had the right to a written death? Certainly not all the dead, but only some of them, the more authoritative male members of the community, and especially, as has been pointed out, the oldest. This right was gradually extended to women (4 percent in the seventeenth century, 28 percent in the early nineteenth century), to younger members of the community (beginning with the end of the eighteenth century) and to the men of the urban and rural middle and lower middle class, beginning with ministers of religion. Thus, even in communities where many, if not quite all adults were able to read and write, the right to a written death remained restricted to the few, and only gradually did it spread to larger circles of people, to wider categories of citizens. This confirms the picture of the ancien régime in the Western world, where it was not enough to have learned to read and write to have the right to written death. Nor was this related, at least in America, to the cost of gravestones. Given their crude fashioning, they certainly cost no more than the heirs of a schoolteacher, shopkeeper, or craftsman could afford. As we know, Mozart's body was dumped in the common grave, and nobody, in the Vienna of 1791, raised an eyebrow.

3.   Between the seventeenth century and the eighteenth, there were no stone carvers in the American colonies comparable in profession-

alism and skill to those in Europe. When a monument, such as Canova's memorial to Sir Walter Raleigh, was required, the work was executed in England or elsewhere on the Continent, and then erected in situ. Local workers, however, were employed for the funerary requirements of the local notables and those who had gradually won the right to a written death. These workmen created a startlingly large number of funerary monuments variously described as "primitive" art or "American Baroque" and—ignoring the question of derivation from the analogous English provincial production—they reveal features of style and of technique that had evolved for more than a century and a half in almost total autonomy.

The social function of collective memory that inscribed gravestones took on in the American colonies—then in the United States after the end of the eighteenth century and particularly at the beginning of the nineteenth—is shown by the nature of the practitioners who, in the seventeenth and eighteenth centuries, at least, were not craftsmen specializing solely in this activity. They were "recorders of events" in the sense that, between one tombstone and the next, they also wrote documents, registered births and marriages, and kept diaries. A typical case is that of Joshua Hempstead of Connecticut, who performed a variety of activities apart from that of carving tombstones. He was justice of the peace, officiated at weddings, registered contracts, and, in his writing mania, kept an extremely detailed diary for decades.

What counted for these American stone carvers was the text. Images are present only as ornament or comment; the center of the stone is always occupied by text, often prolix and generally structured as a biographical section (historical, properly speaking) and a devotional section with biblical quotations. Considered as a whole, in any cemetery, these texts constitute a detailed history book of the community and an important product of the isolated, limited, but organic culture, deeply marked by the reading of sacred books, of the American Protestants and of the Puritans in particular.

Since it was the text that counted most, it was natural that it received much attention and the largest area of space. Even in the simplest and most crudely executed stones there is obvious concern to write as clearly as possible. Particular care was devoted to giving the letters a deep cut, both so that they would stand out and to ensure that they lasted over time.

4.   In this particularly American production—isolated, and with all the characteristics of a sharp stylistic "deviance" from models of "educated" funerary carving—skilled practitioners very soon appeared. These were men of remarkable personality who rehandled graphic forms with ability and inventiveness, exploiting different sources of inspiration that certainly included, apart from their remote English matrix, illustrated printed books, posters, and the products of calligraphy.

During the seventeenth century, a generic majuscule in the Renaissance tradition was widely employed, as it was in contemporary Great Britain. It was deeply cut, ornamented with ligatures between adjacent letters, and sometimes with curious letters, such as an *A* with a triangular cross stroke and an upside-down *N*.

One of the most important stone carvers in the last quarter of the seventeenth century was the anonymous "Charlestown Carver" of Boston, active beginning in 1678. He was a skillful fashioner of gravestones with deeply cut, well-spaced capitals, arranged in modules of different size to fit the partitioning of the text. His particularity was the frequent use of ligatures, fanciful extensions of the foot of the uprights of Arabic numerals, and use of the ampersand. A little later comes another original Boston stone carver, the Quaker William Munford (d. 1718), who was also a tinker, a builder, and a roof mender. He used only capitals, deeply cut and richly decorated with forked ends on the uprights. His stones are well laid out and the letters, though heavy and square, are elegantly carved. He may have had some connection with the anonymous carver who signed himself J.N., to whom we owe the splendid Boston gravestone (1697–98) of Ruth Carter, with its eight lines of deeply cut capitals and accentuated forking of the uprights, and other gravestones from the early eighteenth century.

One of the most important families of New England stone carvers was the Lamsons. The founder, Joseph, an Englishman from Ipswich, was active into the early eighteenth century and died in 1722. He was one of the first to use the round minuscule alongside the majuscule in American funerary epigraphy. One of his sons, Nathanael, carved some of the most handsome gravestones of the early eighteenth century, including that of the Reverend Jonathan Pierpont of Wakefield, using slender capitals for the name and various sizes of minuscule for the thirteen lines of the dense, two-part text. Nathanael and his brother Caleb also introduced a cursive minuscule into American funerary epigraphy that is clearly inspired by both English and book models. The stone-carving activity of the Lamson family continued up to 1808.

The Stevens were another such family, long active in Newport. Known from 1705 onward, they carved elegant and well-executed minuscules. The third of them, John III, wrote verse and used cursive in his epigraphs. A remarkable stone carver by the name of Nathanael Fuller, a descendant of the doctor who sailed on the Mayflower, was active in Plympton between 1698 and 1750. About three hundred of his gravestones have survived, written in a strong capital featuring heavy ornamental forks. Though self-taught, he managed to establish a school. He continued the tradition of the death's head carved on the upper part of the tombstone, but inserted a tiny human head inside it, perhaps to symbolize the immortal soul.

5.   Around the mid-eighteenth century, the production of tombstones increased in volume throughout the American colonies, and the right to a written death spread to categories of people until then excluded, while the number of inscribed gravestones dedicated to the young gradually increased. Concurrent with these phenomena, and particularly during the fourth decade of the century, there were remarkable changes, not only in the graphic aspect of inscriptions, but also in the decoration and structuring of texts. The head of a plump, smiling, and winged cherub took the place of the winged skull of gloomy Puritan tradition. Gravestones began to carry a likeness of the dead, at first in abstract form, but then portrayed in increasingly realistic fashion, and texts became ever longer and more complex, containing biographical data, eulogies, quotations, maxims, and verse compositions.

William Codner (d. 1769), a remarkable stone carver from Boston, was active around the midcentury. He fashioned gravestones of a cultivated sort, with coats of arms, plant motifs, and well-designed texts in round minuscule with ornamental elements and monumental capitals. As cursive became ever more widespread, an oval disc in relief, taken from European models, also established itself as frame for the writing.

In the last quarter of the eighteenth century, symbolic motifs such as the urn and the willow, introduced directly from Great Britain and Romantic in flavor, appeared and rapidly established themselves. Meanwhile, formulas of lamentation and mourning appeared in the text. Another minor form of written record of the dead, what are known as "mourning pictures," appeared during the same period. Funerary scenes sketched in pen and brush or printed using various techniques (including lithography, especially after 1820) were headed with the formula "Sacred to the memory of" followed by the name. Initially manifestations of private and familial piety (some are embroidered on cloth), these funerary manifestos soon became an industrial product and borrowed such European neoclassical motifs as the altar and the urn.

The adoption of these stylistic elements during the first decades of the newborn United States, the ever more obvious imitation of contemporary English models, and the progressive improvement in the artistic level of native production signaled the abandonment by American funerary art of an old and highly original colonial tradition and its graphic and stylistic expressions, though for over a century and half they had represented an autonomous and organic answer to the problem of how to write death in an undoubtedly literate but isolated and monocultural society.

Ordering the Corpses, Ordering
the Writing

1.   During the first half of the eighteenth century, Europeans began to talk about dead bodies and tombs more frankly than they ever had before. A particular literature of tombs and cemeteries developed, steeped in pathos and morbid sentiment. It was a moment when the status of tombs and funerary writing was once again radically modified. One after the other, all the European cultures joined in this general movement, but the decisive impulse came from the new secular mentality in France, the widespread result of Enlightenment thinking, and from English pre-Romanticism, exuberant in its creation of new emblems of sentimentality and pathos.

Though the history is well known, it is worth giving a quick summary here. One might start with events in France, and particularly in Paris, relating to the burial of the dead and the relocation of urban cemeteries. As early as 1737–38, the Parlement of Paris appointed two doctors to investigate the condition and hygiene of the city's cemeteries, especially the largest of them, Les Saints Innocents, where all kinds of activity went on, with people trading, enjoying their amusements, and even living there. In 1745 a *Lettre sur les sépultures dans les églises*, written by Abbot Charles Gabriel Porée, spoke of the hazard to public health inherent in the presence of graves in inhabited centers. Twenty years later, another inquiry on the same question, again voted by the Parlement of Paris, recommended—despite the explicit opposition of the Parisian clergy—an end to the practice of burial within the city and the creation of extramural cemeteries. On May 21, 1765, the Parlement banned burial within the walls, except for clergy and those who were willing to pay a considerable sum for the privilege.

Behind these moves lay an essentially secular current of thought eager to rationalize and defuse the relationship with death, rid it of religious fear and awe, and, all in all, wall off the world of the dead—who were to lie and sleep in peace—from that of the living, who might thus escape ideological blackmail and bodily closeness to a congregation of the dead administered and represented by the clergy.

On March 10, 1776, came a royal decree prohibiting burial in churches and ordering the removal of cemeteries beyond the city walls. This was followed on the first of December 1780 by an ordinance from the Parlement of Paris closing the cemeteries within the city. And finally, between 1785 and 1787—at night, in a macabre and highly charged atmosphere—the great cemetery of Les Saints Innocents was gradually emptied.

The notion spread rapidly through Europe. On June 26, 1786, Joseph II of the Hapsburgs decreed similar legislation, and in 1785, 1786, and 1787, analogous decrees were put out by the Spanish monarchy.

The French Revolution only quickened the pace. The still-unfinished church of Sainte-Geneviève was transformed into a pantheon of republican luminaries. A decree given out by Fouché on September 19, 1793, allowed only those who had deserved well of the fatherland to have "a shaped stone" on their tomb and ordered that the words "Death is an everlasting sleep" be written over the entrance to cemeteries.

In 1801–2, Napoleon commanded new *extra muros* cemeteries for Paris, those of Montparnasse, Montmartre, and Le Père Lachaise. On June 12, 1804, it was forbidden to construct monuments in cemeteries. In Italy, the notion provoked an argument that set state against state, city against city, intellectuals against clergy. One of its manifestations was the *Saggio intorno al luogo del seppellire* (Venice, 1774). In it, Scipione Piattoli, an admirer of the Enlightenment, openly supported the cause in rationalistic arguments that invoked "the indispensable necessity for public Cemeteries to be outside the city" (p. 77) and a return to cemeteries as a restoration of the "customs of our ancestors" (p. 86). That same year, Francesco III d'Este, duke of Modena, banned burials from the city and gave his support to the establishment of the extramural cemetery of San Cataldo, despite the opposition of the local nobility. Modesto Rastrelli, in his *Storia dei riti funebri e delle sepolture antiche e moderne ed osservazioni sui nuovi Campi Santi* (Florence, 1784), made a violent attack on the religious superstitions linked to the cult of the dead. And at the start of the new century, when the Napoleonic Code began to be applied in Italy, the quarrel broke out afresh.

So it was that between the Enlightenment and the eve of the Revolution, during the upheaval itself and on into the Napoleonic Wars, in the face of opposition, violent outbursts, and protests from the people and the clergy, amid grotesque and macabre episodes, the expulsion of the dead took place, and they were exiled from the living fabric of the city to be set apart in cities of their own. These became crowded with a new way of writing death, obsessively repeated in the egalitarian multiplication of tombs. Meanwhile, in their turn, the cities were being deprived of what had been a continuous cultural stimulus— fresh examples of funerary writing—with which the new generations, the new civilization of the century that was arising, were already losing familiarity.

2.   While this was taking place in continental Europe, in England, where the coexistence of inhabited centers, churches, and graveyards was already an established fact, the forms of death and burial that were to shape the culture of the century were assuming a markedly sentimental aspect, mediated and spread by some outstandingly successful literary products that show a considerable awareness of funerary writing.

The first instance in this canon of graveyard literature was a poem, significantly entitled *The Grave*, by the Presbyterian pastor Robert Blair, first published in London in 1743 and several times reprinted. The luxury London edition of 1808, illustrated with twelve etchings by Luigi Schiavonetti from drawings by William Blake and with a preface by Henry Fuseli, is some indication of its success. More than eight hundred people subscribed to the volume, including the queen of England herself.

Though Blair's poem was the prototype of the genre, it did not have the good fortune of others that followed in the subsequent few years. Edward Young's celebrated poem, *The Complaint; Or, Night Thoughts on Life, Death, and Immortality*, published between 1742 and 1745, a long meditation on matters funerary, had wide success in Europe, while *Meditations Among the Tombs*, by another clergyman, James Hervey, a composition in poetic prose more directly linked to the theme of the tomb, published for the first time in London in 1746, was also very successful. There was, finally and most famously, Thomas Gray's *Elegy Written in a Country Churchyard*, in which the author muses over the simple decoration of the stones and the names and ages of the dead crudely inscribed there by an "unletter'd Muse." Though one might take Gray's title to be pointing up the importance of funerary writing, it closes with an improbable epitaph of twelve whole lines in an altogether generic tone.

The *Elegy*, first published in London in 1751 and reprinted five times that same year (plus four appearances in literary magazines), was a sensational success in Europe, translated six times between 1761 and 1770, thirteen times between 1771 and 1780 and—indicative of the period—as many as twenty times between 1791 and 1800. It held its ground in the new century: sixteen translations were made between 1801 and 1810, and fifteen between 1811 and 1820.

3.   Ugo Foscolo was well aware of this literary tradition and held no high opinion of it. Defending his poem *I sepolcri* from its critics in 1807, he wrote as follows: "Young and Hervey meditated on Christian tombs: the purpose of their books is resignation to death and the solace of the afterlife; and the tombs of Protestants sufficed for Protestant preachers. Gray wrote as a philosopher; the purpose of his elegy is to reason the darkness of life and the tranquillity of death, hence, a country churchyard suffices him." In contrast to the English school, Foscolo insists his poem has social, indeed explicitly political, aims. His muse cannot content herself with so narrow a range, or let herself be tainted by religious sentimentality: "the author," he continues, "considers tombs politically, and his purpose is to stir the political emulation of the Italians by the example of nations that honor the memory and the tombs of great men." The history of *I sepolcri*, one of the most famous and most original poems in European funerary literature, is a long one, and not altogether clear. What is sure is that the poem, 295 lines of direct address to Ippolito Pindemonte, first saw light in Brescia in 1807 and probably already existed in written form in 1806. Years later, Foscolo was himself to claim that it was occasioned by the Napoleonic provisions forbidding "the burial of the dead in family tombs. . . . According to the dispositions of this new law, all the dead were to be buried, without distinction, in public cemeteries outside the city walls; and the size of tombstones was prescribed and epitaphs were subject to the revision and approval of magistrates."

What stirred Foscolo's indignation was the rationally egalitarian bent inherent in French post-Revolutionary legislation, putting all the dead theoretically on the same plane, making their funerary memory equivalent, and brutally limiting the freedom of the pen through a threatened censorship of epitaphs. From the start, *I sepolcri* claims the right of the "great" to a fitting written memorial as a social value and explicitly refers to it several times:

> What comfort for lost days
> Is a stone that distinguishes mine from the countless
> Bones death sows by land and sea?
>
> (ll. 13–15)

And again: "and may a stone keep the name" (l. 38); and on the subject of Parini: "No shade for him the city set within its wall . . . no stone or word" (ll. 72–75). The written memory of the dead—or rather of some of the dead—is thus of social and political importance, but not in the ways proper to medieval and Baroque tradition:

> Not always did gravestones serve as paving
> For churches; nor the incense-wrapped stench
> Of corpses pollute the supplicants,
> Nor were the cities grim with pictured skeletons.
>
> (ll. 104–8)

There is another model, that of the cemetery as garden, which Foscolo sees both in its classical and English form—dear to "British maidens" (ll. 131–32)—the force of his polemic here compacting two situations really too dissimilar for comparison.

As we well know, Foscolo's fears were misplaced. Equality in burial and the silencing of funerary writing did not happen, and for very good reasons. Despite the results of mass literacy and revolutionary ideology, the ruling classes managed to hold on to the privilege of written death expressed in particular and distinctive forms. Once again, this came about through the adoption of a graphic and textual language of funerary writing, based directly on classical models, radically new compared with both the tradition of the seventeenth and eighteenth centuries and the impoverished and widespread productions of northern religious cultures. Neoclassical funerary writing chose the model—favored by Foscolo—of the "sublime" memorial, compressed into a few words and quickly taken in, set up in the open and consisting of restrained, figured structures. The ordering of the dead thus went along with an ordinance imposed on writing, and the purpose was to maintain differences so that "great men" might continue to be honored with monuments and in written words—even if in forms that were continually renewed—as they, and only they, had for so many centuries been entitled.

～

4.   In 1781, exactly 127 years after the publication of that manifesto of Baroque epigraphy, Emanuele Tesauro's *Il cannocchiale aristotelico*, the countermanifesto of neoclassical epigraphy, *De stilo inscriptionum latinarum libri III* by Stefano Antonio Morcelli, was published in Rome. Its first page curtly describes Tesauro's inscriptions as "monsters" and goes on to condemn the current epigraphical style as "licentiousness in writing and playacting" (p. 2). The barbarities and ignorance of the Latin of the age just passed, its wretched versifying, foreign importations, and characters distorted by uncertain *ductus*, are lamented (p. ix), as are epitaphs so extravagantly long that no one can read them in their entirety (p. 327).

What does Morcelli propose instead? He suggests a return to a style so old, indeed, so ancient, that it was ironically new: a pure and simple return to classical forms on the level of text and formula, as well as on the graphic level proper. In particular, he recommends the adoption of large, squared capitals of different sizes according to the Roman models of the age of Trajan and Hadrian, and goes on to conclude that "nothing can be written in a more orderly way, nothing can be read more rapidly" (p. 462).

The truth of the matter is that Morcelli, like Foscolo later, was not one of the forerunners. He followed and reinforced changes, backed them with words, examples, and suggestions, but the shift toward a clearer epigraphy for funerary (and other) purposes—writing terser and more readable than that of Baroque epigraphy—had been under way throughout Europe from at least the thirties and forties of the century, and was invading even the sphere of book production. As early as 1757, the Englishman John Baskerville, who had begun as a carver of gravestones—singular coincidence!—and then became a businessman, after years of experiment printed his admirable corpus of the works of Virgil in a new, classicizing character. Later, in Parma, Giovan Battista Bodoni designed and used for decades a heavy Roman majuscule character with strongly contrasting thick and thin strokes that was to become the ideal of nineteenth-century Italian and European letter design.

Funerary writing everywhere was moving in the same direction, gradually abandoning Baroque styles and fragmented and fanciful layouts. In one of the most famous European tombs of the eighteenth century, that constructed (beginning in 1762) for Maurice of Saxony, marshal of France, in the church of Saint Thomas in Strasbourg by the great Jean-Baptiste Pigalle, despite a still highly dramatic scene with lions, banners, and figures in tragic poses, the classicizing writing dominates and regulates the whole. The text, laid out in eight lines and arranged in two sections, is inscribed on the pyramidal load-bearing structure of the monument and is once again, as in antiquity and the Renaissance, the central element in the composition. Similarly, in the tomb of Ferdinand VI, king of Spain, erected after 1761 in Santa Barbara in Madrid by Francesco Sabatini and Francisco Gutierrez, the inscription, carved on a plaque of classical shape, strongly contrasts with the structure of a monument still richly Baroque in feeling. One can see the same contrast in the funerary wall monument of Francesco Algarotti—the subject of lively polemic when it was erected in the Camposanto of Pisa in 1764—where the division of the written parts, all strictly classical in layout and graphic style, hardly fits the bright colors and the generally late-Renaissance mold.

Antonio Canova was the artist who radically changed the arrangement of writing on tombs. On the numerous funerary monuments he designed and executed and on tombstones scattered throughout the churches of Rome and other Italian cities, he brilliantly reconstructed the placing, extent, distribution, and presence of writing itself. Among these examples, which Roberto Longhi ungenerously described as the "cemeterial blunders" of a "stillborn sculptor," there are splendid proofs of a new way of understanding the relationship of writing with death and with the dead, beginning with the large funerary monument to Clement XIV, executed between 1783 and 1787 in the church of Santi Apostoli in Rome, where the writing, classically restricted to just the name and title, is arranged centrally on the sarcophagus and partially hidden, in elegant reference to Bernini, by a female statue. Further evidence is the later mausoleum of Clement XIII in San Pietro, finished in 1792, an autograph sketch of which shows writing set either side of a tondo, with bold splitting of the name. But above all there is the large mausoleum in the Augustiner Kirche in Vienna of Maria Cristina of Austria, wife of Albert, duke of Saxony-Teschen, erected between 1798 and 1805 and judged by Stendhal "the foremost of existing tombs." The large pyramidal monumental structure has the writing split between a circular legend in the tondo containing the likeness of the deceased and the imposing, large raised capitals of gilded metal, set on the central door and laid out in antique fashion in two lines, a record of the husband who commissioned it: "VXORI. OPTIMAE / ALBERTVS."

Even in Canova's more modest tomb monuments there is always inventiveness. Take, for example, the motif of writing carved on a pillar surmounted by the bust of the deceased that he employed in the memorial to Angelo Emo in the Arsenale of Venice and in that of Giacomo Volpato in the church of Santi Apostoli in Rome. Or again, the motif of unfinished writing on the slab bearing the inscription, exemplified in the tombstone of Nicola Antonio Giustiniani in the Museo Civico of Padua. Or again, the carefully laid-out arrangement of the seven-line central inscription on the Stuart monument (1819) in Saint Peter's.

Canova's ability to satisfy the neoclassical desire for sober and archaistic funerary writing in original ways depended to some extent on his adoption of such Baroque motifs as writing hidden or broken off, and on suggestions from other sources, such as the inscribed pillar, more paleo-Christian than classical. But it also depended on his restoring writing to the center of the monument and reducing to the minimum—not its presence, which is always imposing—but the length of the text, in line with Morcelli's ideas. His work, which was known from Russia to the United States, influenced the funerary sculpture of the Western Hemisphere for decades.

5.   In 1828, the cautious Abbot Antonio Cesari, a purist and teacher of purists, wrote in some wonder: "Are you aware that the learned are now eager to bring back Italian Epigraphy? Giordani is one of them." Apart from the efforts of Pietro Giordani, there was in fact a growing movement during the second decade of the nineteenth century to reintroduce the epigraph in Italian, culminating in the *Discorso sulla epigrafia italiana* with which Francesco Orioli prefaced an 1826 collection of Italian inscriptions by different authors. The project brought together classicists such as Giordani, motivated by love of the purity, richness, and versatility of their mother tongue, and Romantics who opposed the excessive and exclusive use of Latin and advocated the shared language of the people. As with Latin, there could, of course,

be only one model, the classical one reproposed by Morcelli, to which both Orioli and Giordani explicitly pressed for a return.

According to Pietro Giordani, inscriptions in the vernacular should be short, clear, effective, decorous, and above all, simple, without inversions, transpositions, obsolete terms, or Latinisms, and he went on to warn that "when we give ourselves importance, it is then done with negligence or with affectation." But what he most opposed was excessive length of the text: "I am extremely anxious for brevity," he declared. "When one writes not on paper, but on marble, one must be very parsimonious with syllables and letters, not just words."

According to Antonio Cesari, the lack of models remained a problem: "since we don't have exemplars of the Italian epigraphical style, it is a roll of the dice." But Giordani replies, "This genre can still be called new, because it belongs to few, because it has not been successfully attempted." And he and others such as Luigi Muzzi and Giuseppe Manuzzi had soon provided multiple examples. Cesari in time came around and composed epigraphs in Italian to match those in Latin that he never ceased to love and produce.

In the space of a few decades, Italian cemeteries (and even churches, where allowed) filled with funerary inscriptions in Italian, differing in size and nature, but in terms of formulas, sentiments, and content, all new compared with the Latin examples from the period immediately prior.

The novelty was mainly visible in the script—the large, heavy, and sharply contrasted Bodonian majuscule already mentioned, which made every epigraph look like the title page of a book or an official wall poster—and the text, which, after the very early period, by the thirties and forties tended to be long and complex, dynamically structured in several sections. Meanwhile, the new concepts gave pride of place to social values, familial virtues, and financial flair.

The novelty of this Italian vernacular epigraphy also lay in the fact that it was largely middle-class. And the attention it paid to children, young people, and women, until then neglected categories of the dead and now to be immortalized in written death, was also middle-class and new. Let us take a collection of 129 inscriptions by Pietro Giordani published in Rome in 1834. It contains as many as 39 (30 percent) funerary inscriptions devoted to women, 8 to children and 7 to "maids and youths." The inscriptions composed by Giordani, the century's most fortunate and successful writer of vernacular epigraphs, reveal another characteristic of the genre: the appearance during the thirties and forties of the nineteenth century—when the text became longer and more discursive—of pathetic formulas of lament and appeal in harmony with middle-class mentality and behavior and very remote from Morcelli's models : "Oh pain, oh pain" ; "Oh painful vanity of the world!" They also carefully specified the cause of death, whether sickness or anything else. The inclusion of these concrete, realistic elements in funerary epigraphy was another novelty introduced by these new people, people fond of information, knowledge, full of questions and curious about the death of others of their kind, over whom they continued to mourn in human fashion as long as written traces of mourning remained.

Vernacular funerary epigraphy represented a further stage in the extension of the right of written death to strata until then excluded. Giordani, a secular illuminist and democrat, was already by 1813 demanding that the poor should have "some very modest and inexpensive memorial to cover their bones; on condition the writing make clear it was done by the Municipality." And he goes on to add that "perhaps the time will come when this is understood and pleases, and becomes the custom."

Despite Giordani's generous view, much time was still required. The situation of the poor was very different, and in 1833—while Giordani was still alive and Canova only recently dead—Belli set it out with all his usual rawness in the sonnet *Li morti de Roma*:

THE DEAD OF ROME

The dead that's of the common ruck—
mid the buggered lot of all and one—
go afternoon and wail their luck
to'ards a hole that swallows them.
While t'others with their pinchbeck
seal of gentlemen and whoresons,
are nicer, have the shitty gall to duck
the sun and in the dark go travel on.
And then there's a third sort of guest,
another species of the dead, that walks
uncandled and uncoffined to his rest.
That's us, Clementina, t'other folks,
small fry from the market stall all messed,
on the midden in the morning we get hoicked.

The Middle Class and Its Writing

I.

And then I love cemeteries, because they are monstrous cities, prodigiously inhabited. Think of how many dead there are in this small space, of all the generations of Parisians that are lodged here forever, troglodytes enclosed in their small tombs once and for all, in their little holes covered by a stone or marked by a cross, while the living occupy so much space and make so much noise, the imbeciles . . . in cemeteries there are monuments almost as interesting as in museums. . . . And I set myself to reading the epitaphs. This, for example, is the most diverting thing in the world.

Such is the view expressed by Guy de Maupassant in his well-known story "Les tombales."

To go into a nineteenth-century European monumental cemetery means entering upon a great universe of writing, encountering graphic experiences of the most diverse kind, feeling the effect of the most jumbled and yet most continuous presence of exhibited written testimony imaginable. Inevitably, one's first reaction is rejection, one's immediate judgment is of having wandered into a mad and muddled graphic chaos. But when one actually takes a closer look, the chaos has its own stable order, social and hierarchic, and follows the dictates of a geometric grid within which certain artifacts work as signposts, serve as landmarks and points of reference, reflecting in the immobile fixity of stone and metal, of writing and images, the seemingly chaotic and uncontrollable movement—but in reality controlled and regulated activity—of the society of the living. The middle-class nineteenth-century cemetery is its marvelous mirror image.

Within these petrified cities of the dead, the distribution of burial space, and therefore of space for the display of writing, is rigidly programmed into the actual physical structure of the complex, the zoning regulations of which distinguish areas of privilege from those common to all. However, artistic and graphic expression within the program was left entirely free; choice of this or that model was a matter of chance; selection of the craftsman, of materials, of the amplitude and structuring of the texts, of their placing, fragmentation and division was left to the client. And the clients made use of their freedom by constructing memorial monuments to their dead with the same artistic taste, the same abhorrence of the void, the same love of "modernity" that filled middle-class apartments with every kind of furniture, ornament, and trinket, to the point of saturation. And the same was true on the graphic level, where the model was no longer the book or the epigraphical tradition of the past, but the explosion in advertising that filled the roads of the European and North American metropolis with posters on which the most variegated styles of writing, upright and cursive, bold and Bodoni, Gothic and Renaissance Roman, mixed and mingled in one vast graphic bedlam.

This graphic confusion was abetted by the diversity of materials used and by the fanciful schemes of the various monumental structures. As early as the forties and fifties of the nineteenth century, the old epigraphical order had been shattered, and funerary monuments made room for writing in diverse modes and styles. Especially toward the end of the century, metal was much used for chapels, altars, and supports in the shape of candelabra with lecterns on which written scrolls were propped. Often, metal went along with glass. The client was given free rein, and the monumental styles were all-embracing. The early twentieth century provides examples of neo-Gothic, pseudo-Renaissance, Romanesque, Byzantine and Art Nouveau. The writing kept pace by adopting a variety of shapes for letters, colors, layouts, and abbreviations. Some examples even have ancient "rustic" capitals, and the "Greek-style letters" used in the Po Valley during the early fifteenth century make a reappearance.

2.   The places set aside for these complex and programmed displays of funerary writing were the great urban cemeteries of the larger cities of continental Europe. In Paris, for example, these were Le Père Lachaise, Montmartre, and Montparnasse, which, given the expansion of the metropolis, soon found themselves within the city boundaries; in Mi-

lan, the monumental cemetery; in Rome, the Campo Verano; in Genoa, the famous Staglieno cemetery, still a goal today for awestruck tourists.

In these cities of death and remembrance constructed by the European urban middle class in self-celebration, the main purpose of the monumental-graphic structure was to give positive identity to the social group, that is, to the family as nucleus and its individual members, distinguished by a common surname. In the contemporary commercial and industrial field, this was also the goal of advertising, designed to distinguish individual products even—and especially—when they were similar or analogous. The choice of discordant styles, of a variety of scripts, of variegated materials and colors, the extravagance in ornament, served precisely to distinguish the dead one from another, to brand them and underline their social and family connections, to prevent their obliteration in the leveling confusion of anonymous death.

The immediate distinction required by this middle-class death, at once particularizing and identical in its diversity, was based on an extremely meticulous realism, a realism embodied in the effigy, obsessively detailed in the particulars of face, clothes, shoes, cape, hat, and lace of the deceased and their dear ones; in individual portraits, at first sculpted or painted on slate or metal, then photographically reproduced on ceramic material; in the long biographical text summarizing the career and recording the merits and virtues of the deceased, sometimes, in an excess of candor, even giving out the cause of death. These texts, rendered more pathetic by obvious but emphatic formulas detailing the distress and mourning of the living, provide portraits of the middle class that are both true and false—industrious husbands and fathers, faithful, honest, fortunate in their careers, in business or the professions; wives and mothers exemplary for their domestic virtues, for love of their children, for their devoutness. A great deal of attention is paid to the untimely death of children—gratified by many inscriptions of their own—and of young people. A collection of epitaphs dating from between 1830 and 1880 in the Pellegrini cemetery in Naples makes clear that some monuments had long verse compositions and that the effusion often could occupy most of the space available.

In Italy, the most solidly and clearly middle-class cemetery in this sense was the Staglieno in Genoa, designed in 1840. An entire industrial, business, financial, and professional class chose to get itself immortalized there in a supreme triumph of kitsch. According to Corrado

Maltese, "the inscriptions and figures could not help mirroring the sentimental alibis, the *pudeurs*, the ideology (the values of self-sacrifice, resignation, and industry) and the hypocrisy of the ruling classes." There, as in the Campo Verano in Rome, the modern and discordant Art Nouveau alphabet sometimes slips in among Byzantine, Romanesque, neo-Gothic and pseudo-Renaissance scripts. There, as everywhere else, over time there was a growth in the number of family funerary chapels, a certain sign of decorum, success, respectability, and economic prosperity, proudly inscribed with the surname alone, as if they were shops, factories, or private banks.

It is not surprising, therefore, that the reaction of a spirit as independent and mordant as Giuseppe Giusti to the first signs of this explosion of epigraphical rhetoric should be repulsion. His *Il mementomo* denounces the falsity of middle-class funerary practice and its formulas, its obvious social inequality, its absurdity and the "word tinkers or epigraph inkers" who traded in it. And he violently rejects the idea of any kind of written memorial for himself:

> By God, the stone
> scares me stiff.
> In my will
> I'll leave it as a gift
> that I go among cabbages
> without *here lies*;
> let your neighbor
> rot in peace.

But even he got his fine "stone," composed by none other than Gino Capponi, and we will never know what he thought of it.

---

3.   Over the last 40 years of the nineteenth century and the first two decades of this century, bourgeois society had to face and deal with the problem of the written memory of the dead on a new basis as the result of three concomitant factors. The first was a constant rise in population almost everywhere, with the consequent and decisive victory of the values of life over death. This went along with increasingly widespread literacy, now for the first time within the reach of the lower classes, at least those living in cities, and for the first time a mass phenomenon. The third factor was the unheard-of slaughter caused on the battlefields of wars of destruction by the invention of rapid-fire

weapons. The cycle began with the American Civil War of 1861–65 and reached its peak, in terms of military losses, during the Great European War of 1914–18. In the American Civil War, the Union dead came to three hundred and sixty thousand; the Confederacy lost two hundred and fifty-eight thousand. Given these appalling figures, the Union government decided—and it was the first time in history since the listing of the Attic war dead in the fifth century B.C.—that all the fallen had a right to a separate tomb and a written record of their death, whether they were officers or simple soldiers, whether their identity was known or not.

Up until then, Western society had reacted to mass death—caused less by man than by epidemics—without changing the unwritten laws reserving the right to a written death to the upper classes, and thus to certain categories of people only. The scale of the phenomenon—the Black Death, for example, killed half of Europe in the fourteenth century—did nothing to alter the range of the individual written funerary record. Larger and more numerous common graves fulfilled the need. In response to the internecine slaughter that had profoundly divided the nation for five years, the United States, by then a largely literate country characterized by political institutions of a democratic kind, instead acknowledged the right of the fallen to individual funerary memory, though certain hierarchical distinctions were kept in the actual constructions. The example was catching. In Europe, after the bloodletting of the Franco-Prussian War of 1870–71, monuments to the war dead and military cemeteries were established in the two countries involved. In Paris, at the Ecole des Beaux-Arts itself, Henri Chapu built a curious and ornate monument in a vaguely neoclassical style to the memory of the artists fallen in the war, with the names inscribed in two long columns.

The Great War of 1914–18 was the greatest military slaughter in human history. Entire generations of young European males were massacred, draining the lifeblood of all the countries involved beyond hope of remedy. The collective mind was profoundly struck by this mass sacrifice, and the pain was exorcized not by taking refuge in oblivion and repression, but by the rhetoric of patriotism, by celebrating the heroic virtues of the dead and the value of the sacrifice they had offered on behalf of their country. The fallen, all "heroes" now, were recorded with remarkable unanimity in all the warring countries in two orders of inscribed funerary memory: mass military cemeteries, where the identified and the unknown dead were buried together, and the shared celebratory monuments erected in every town and city in memory of the fallen of each neighborhood, quarter, and district. Their written memory was thus doubled, set up in their birthplace "in absentia" of the dead and "in praesentia" where the bloodshed had occurred. It is calculated that between 1920 and 1922, around thirty thousand commemorative monuments were erected in France alone.

4.   The real shrines of this new form of mass written funerary memory were the great war cemeteries. They were laid out everywhere according to ideological designs, shaped by uniformity, geometrical simplicity, spatial harmony, anti-individualism, and the strong and direct bond of the single "hero" with his local community. The writing is reduced to the minimum for each of the dead, but it is obsessively present when considered overall, and what renders its presence still more oppressive is the absolute uniformity, the layout always equal, the same number of lines on each plaque, the data repeated for each of the dead, the throng of names clustered side by side on wall monuments, on steps, on exedras.

The largest war cemetery in Italy is Redipuglia (Gorizia), designed by Giovanni Greppi and Giannino Castiglioni, which lodges the remains of 100,187 soldiers, of whom 39,857 are identified and 60,330 unknown. The names of the former are inscribed on the 22 steps holding the loculi, with bronze plates bearing information. Below the steps towers the large monolith marking the remains of Emanuele Filiberto, duke of Aosta, commander of the Third Army. The solution adopted by Ghino Venturi for the cemetery of Oslavia, which holds 20,760 identified soldiers and 30,000 unknown, was original in its repetitiveness. The unknown soldiers are buried in three great tombs; the names of those identified run around the internal walls of four enormous towers, in columns bearing thirteen lines of writing each.

In Redipuglia, the sense of sacrifice is underlined by grotesque inscriptions dedicated to the unknown dead, steeped in naive, jingoistic rhetoric of the following kind: "That my name not be seen is best / if in the soil I defended I now rest," or "The tomb my name cannot tell / but God blesses it and knows it well." In the temple shrine in Udine, completed in 1940, where 21,518 of the Great War dead are buried, a Latin inscription records the unknown soldiers: "and we gave our name along with our blood to the fatherland."

And yet even in this harmoniously and uniformly egalitarian cele-bration of the supreme sacrifice for the fatherland, hierarchy manages to get itself respected. Senior ranks, particularly generals, are buried apart. Some of them, such as the duke of Aosta already mentioned, have the right to a large individual monument. In fact, the whole op-eration of memorializing the slaughter was everywhere (and particu-larly in Italy) designed and executed under the supervision and the di-rection of the upper ranks of the armed forces, who stamped it with their ideology, values, and self-justification, perverting the memory of the victims into a celebration of themselves, the survivors who were re-sponsible. The outcome was a colossal bureaucratic operation of reg-istration in exhibited writing immediately recalling the book necrolo-gies of the medieval religious community discussed earlier. But in the case of the *Libri viventium* (i.e., of the dead who had won true life) the recorders had no responsibility whatsoever for the deaths involved, and, indeed, given their ideology, took death to be the antecedent con-dition of a better life. This was certainly not the case with the funerary practices linked to the great military massacres of this century, which had their origin instead in the need to find a social justification for a slaughter imposed particularly on the lower middle classes, and to ex-orcize its terrible memory.

This justification and exorcism must have seemed impossible from a rational standpoint. Indeed, in 1915, a European thinker of the stature of Sigmund Freud could state in his "Thoughts for the Times on War and Death" that in the light of the slaughter of the war, the natural tendency of modern man to "'shelve' death, to eliminate it from life" was revealed as vanity. "Death will no longer be denied; we are forced to believe in him. People really are dying, and now not one by one, but many at a time, often ten thousand in a single day." It was, of course the accep-tance of the obvious fact that led to the conception of a series of strate-gies for manipulating and exorcizing the inadmissible. One of these was the written record, less questionable because of its antiquity, and in this case directly administered by the military and political authorities.

It is no accident that the after terrible collective trauma of the Viet-nam War and its high human, psychological, and political costs to the United States, a solemn and official placatory solution to it was found in the monumental written record of the Vietnam Veterans' Memor-ial in Washington, on which the names of the fifty-eight thousand American dead are inscribed in order on a low wall.

Inherent even in the authoritarian registration "in perpetual memory" of a person's name, there was always a widespread shared acknowledgment and respect for the sacrificed individual. It was precisely this that the Nazis aimed to deny in the concentration camps of the Second World War. Names were replaced by numbers engraved on a pair of metal tags, one attached to the corpse and one to the coffin, when—and it was rare enough—there was a coffin. For those without even this, the promiscuity and anonymity of the common grave had to suffice, as it had done in the not too distant past.

5.   The reaction to the slaughter of war merely put the seal on that generalized extension of the right to a written death that had marked the whole nineteenth century in the West and that reached its acme during the first half of this century. But the fact that in the wake of the right gained by the young victims of the Great War practically all the dead now have a right to a written record of their name in the place where they are laid does not mean that the written registration of death has lost all hierarchical differentiation and finally become democratized as an objectively egalitarian testimony.

Even during the nineteenth century, the upper classes in Western society had found new spaces and new instruments for advertising the death of its members in different and more sophisticated ways. The daily press gave rise to the "obituary" and the "death announcement," which then took their place in the universal concert of "news" of public importance. The former was—and is—the memorial article that a newspaper devotes on its own initiative to people of particular social, cultural, political, and economic importance. The later, in contrast, was—and is—the announcement relatives pay to get published to record the disappearance of a family member and to give information on the time and whereabouts of the funeral. Both are written records of the death of an individual "in absentia," in a printed context that ensures the widest possible diffusion and authority and even (in the archives set aside to preserve them) a certain durability in time. It is hardly rash to suggest that, in publicizing the name of the deceased and his family group, obituaries and announcements fulfilled—and fulfill—the function performed by funerary epigraphy from the Middle Ages to the ancient régime, the period when tombs were located in city churches. It is also worth noticing that these practices coincided

with the spread among the European middle class of the printed visiting card as an instrument of individuation and personal self-celebration. They bore—and bear—a series of elements—name, occupation,
titles, addresses—wherewith the living individual presents himself to
society: a species of modern *cursus honorum* printed on a small piece
of card.

When the obituary and death announcement first became current
and spread, they were a means of communication and self-celebration
among what were all but closed elites. National and local dailies were
everywhere a direct emanation of a ruling class that in any case constituted the largest and most important section of a relatively limited
readership. With time and the spread of literacy and the printed newspaper, the practice of the death notice was adopted by new social
strata, while the parallel increase in readership created a lower-middle-
class and working-class public for the printed record of death used by
the "others." The printed notice of a death used by the upper reaches
of society, with its unchanging structure, list of participants, and funeral details, thus became a sort of miniature novelette offered daily as
instrument of edification and education in reading and meditation for
the middle and lower classes of society.

Though this particular epigraphical "genre" has now spread world-
wide, lack of research makes it unfortunately impossible to catalogue
its formal and textual characteristics and the changes it has undergone
with the completeness one would like. Nevertheless, despite the limi-
tations of the surveys and the necessarily summary nature of comparisons, it remains worthwhile trying to sketch out some of the basic
overall trends.

French newspaper obituaries in the nineteenth and twentieth centuries reveal a society that portrays itself in ideal form and uses in
printed notices the formulas and ideal values present in its contemporary funerary epigraphy. At the start of the twentieth century, the social
range of obituaries widens through its inclusion of women; the number of obituaries devoted to them triples as compared with the period
1839–49.

A survey of different years of the Italian *Corriere della Sera* (1880,
1910, 1925, 1955) reveals a situation in rapid quantitative and qualitative
evolution, up to a certain moment when it becomes all but stationary
in practices and patterns. In January and February 1880, death notices
are very few in number (a general average of one per day) and reserved

almost without exception for the Milanese nobility. Few women are recorded. Notice of a child's death, and that of a doyen of coachmen, including solemn eulogy and valediction, stand out from the rest (January 15 and 16, 1880). The formulas are sober, the kin responsible for the notice scrupulously listed, the place and time of the funerals precisely detailed. On the days following, notices of thanks sometimes appear. Obituaries are few and reserved for nobles and generals.

By January through March 1910, the number of the notices has grown to between two and ten per day, and several separate announcements appear for the same person. The percentage of the notices for women is considerably higher, and professionals (notaries, pharmacists, brokers), businessmen, and shop owners are recorded among the dead. The formulas have become fixed in two analogous schemes, either an impersonal announcement of death ("Yesterday at . . . died"), participation and lists of relatives, details of the funeral and burial; or an announcement by the participant relatives, followed by the funeral details. In March 1925, the picture is more rich and complex; the number has grown to about thirty per day; the dead come from all strata of the city's middle class, including people in industry (managers and accountants), farmers, teachers, a parish priest, and some women. The texts are longer than in the past and include expressions of mourning and generic phrases in praise of the deceased's industriousness, well-spent life, and devoutness.

In January 1955, notices rise to more than eighty per day, many of them plural (28 for a managing director; 35 for a businessman); but apart from the numerical increase, the textual formulation has not changed from those recorded 30 years previously, nor have social origins. Currently, death notices in *Corriere della Sera* number over one hundred per day, but the formulaic structures, length, and purpose have remained as they were, fixed once and for all after the Great War. Comparisons with other linguistic and socio-cultural situations are always difficult, yet despite obvious formal differences, various surveys confirm an impression of the substantial uniformity it is possible to show, for example, between obituaries in the *Corriere della Sera* and in the German *Frankfurter Rundschau* for 1965.

In provincial newspapers, where the number of obituaries is more limited, the space available is greater, and signs of the cross, different font sizes and characters, sometimes even portraits of the dead appear. American notices are richest in information, and for that very reason more ample, though they often omit the precise date of death. But without doubt, the most professionally perfect reports of death are still the English and American newspaper editorial obituaries given by the quality press (*The Times* of London, the *New York Times*) to people of public importance. Following objective standards of information, they manage to include the cause of death and a list of surviving relatives, and through a cataloguing of the stages in the social *cursus honorum* of the dead person (often pictured), they resolve themselves into an optimistic and broadly class-based celebration of the world of the living.

Multiply and Decrease

⁓

1. The custom of recording the memory of one's dead "in absentia" in forms different from those of epigraphical tradition and practice has not been—and is not—exclusive to the upper levels of the middle class. The lower middle classes of society and the elites of small provincial towns remote from the large national dailies also have found ways of using particular types of printed matter to give written notice of their dead. For this they resorted—and still resort—to two curious and widespread products, the wall poster and the so-called *santino*, or holy picture.

Wall posters are particularly to be found in provincial towns and villages and are one of the more visible items in their urban furniture. They are, in general, rectangular in shape, with the writing usually laid out along the long axis within a wide black border dotted with Christian and funerary symbols: thorn-wreathed crosses, broken columns, and praying Madonnas. The texts take the same form as the newspaper announcements: an announcement of death, a list of participants, the deceased's name in large capitals, and the details of the funeral. The graphics are traditional, both in layout and in the choice of characters. The number posted and their distribution around the town depend on the importance of the deceased and his or her family, and hence on what they are willing to pay. Here, too, the amount of space taken by the written record of death is subject to precise restraints of wealth and social position.

The holy picture is a notification of death printed on cardboard, nowadays usually a double-folded card, with an announcement of the death, name, date, and photograph of the deceased—not usually given on the poster—and short texts of a religious nature, either quotations from the Gospels or meditations on the subject of Christian death inspired or composed by the relatives or suggested by the professionals in-volved. The circulation of holy pictures is practically restricted to rela-tives and friends, to the limited circle of people who knew the deceased and who it is supposed would want some form of written memorial as a keepsake. Since the holy picture has its own function as a record and a communication, it is very often used in addition to the wall poster. Here, again, the characters used, the eclectic mix, the images and deco-ration, all religious in nature, make the graphics look several decades out of date. English mourning cards printed in the last 30 years of the nineteenth century also betray a remarkable graphic eclecticism, which often slips into blatant bad taste, with texts in Gothic, cursive, and block letters suffocated by embroidered borders and genre imagery.

2.   Cemetery memorial artifacts—memorials placed where the dead are laid—have been multiplying for some decades now, at least in the funerary practices of the middle and lower classes of society. The grave-stone with biographical data and a picture of the deceased is increas-ingly inscribed with additional texts, done in different techniques and layouts and containing quotations from the Gospels, invocations to the dead, and reflections of a religious nature. Clearly, this structuring of "in praesentia" funerary writing according to different themes and spaces is taking over one of the most widespread types of "in absentia" written record, that of the holy picture already described. It is as if the relatives meant to transform the epigraphical memorial on the loculus and close to the body of the deceased into a holy picture inscribed on hard material and thus perpetuate the messages of regret and hope, the promises of remembrance and appeals for intercession, that make up the texts of the memorial cards.

One also gets the impression that the plurality of writing "in prae-sentia" is in many cases ceasing to be an originary feature, contempo-rary with the burial and programmed from the start, and is becoming a phased process, a progressive accumulation of inscribed material set out and arranged on a grave area that is almost always very limited—that the process itself materializes and symbolizes the continuity in cult prac-tices of the close kin who administer the written record, even if through the mediation and technical collaboration of specialized craftsmen.

Thus, in front of the loculi, next to the slabs, a whole host of ad-ditional micro-epigraphy is appearing on graves. This consists of open books in marble, unrolled scrolls, and smaller or larger rolls offered to the viewer on which naively phrased texts or, more rarely, Gospel quotations are inscribed, usually in ordinary script, that is, school cursive. The motif of the open book, fashionable in French cemeteries in the early decades of this century, appeared and spread in Italy during the thirties and forties, and it still endures with all the tenacity and repetitiveness inherent in forms of popular culture and craft-work practices.

This spontaneous micro-epigraphy is accompanied by imagery and decoration composed of flowers, religious symbols, images of the Virgin and the saints, and plural portraits of the deceased. Very often now, the figured complex is constructed of colored materials, and this marks the return of color to mass funerary epigraphy after a long period in which the austere graphic pattern imposed throughout Europe by neoclassical taste allowed only white or black, though there was a foretaste of it in the early years of the century. Middle-class and popular culture did not embrace this tradition and now denies and reverses its principles by freely and progressively multiplying funerary writing and treating the burial space in a "domestic" way, transforming it into a small home for the deceased, continually written on and brightened with color. The fixed, immutable, and restrained funerary writing required by the classical scheme of nineteenth-century tradition and employed by the upper levels of society now is being challenged by mass production, with an outpouring of private, cursive, spontaneous, variously colored writing, the product of a culture altogether different from the official, learned one, a culture with its own models and its own autonomous means of expression.

3.   Funerary writing takes on peculiar and noteworthy aspects in marginal and exceptional situations, where an absence of models and spontaneous adaptation over a period of time become decisive elements in the graphic and spatial organization of the individual testimony.

The study of tombs in provincial Calabria has brought to light a singular range of graphic and textual archaisms, nineteenth-century scripts, idioms (a capital *I* with dot, an upside-down *Q* for capital *O*), simple mistakes, curious layouts and arrangements, and long, diffuse texts altogether unknown to the usual formulas, embellished with curious biographical details or expressions of mourning with an old-world flavor. The writing is always accompanied by a variety of images, by heart-shaped ornaments with additional inscriptions inside, and there is even an open stone notebook inscribed in minuscule cursive that, in the form of a direct address to the deceased, details the circumstances of his death and seeks his intercession:

> One sunlit morning of
> spring as always
> you left home to go
> to do your duty
> as devoted husband and father.
> But sad was that morning,
> the cruel fate wished for
> who knows by whom, the untimely
> act of nature
> rent you from our hearts,
> leaving them in the profoundest
> pain. Your honored
> sacrifice has stricken all,
> those whom you loved,
> weak is [and] strong, friends
> is [and] enemies, but most of all your
> youth. you are always
> with us, praying the
> lord to give us strength
> is [and] courage and to give you the
> task of watching over us
> at every moment.
> Your loved ones. In m[emory] of . . .
> Renda
> Ferdinando

In the cemetery of San Vito Romano (Rome), a tombstone written in minuscule cursive thus records Augusta Rossi, who died in 1952:

> Wife and exemplary mother
> she reared numerous offspring
> to the struggle for improving
> the standard of living of working people
> patience and uncommon strength
> kept her ideal ever high
> the terrible twenty years of persecution
> were [misspelled] not a fear to her but a spur
> for that reason I think [misspelled] it my duty

as example of posterity t[o] imitate
and of spur to the waverers who is lacking
faith strength ideal.

The tombstone of the famous Roman popular singer Claudio Villa at Rocca di Papa (near Rome) is also in cursive. The words, composed by him, are in raised metal characters and state:

Life is beautiful
death [stinks].

An anonymous censor decided to erase the closing words by chiseling them out.

In analogous situations of cultural marginality, examples of graphic idioms just as curious occur. In the cemetery of Castel Sant' Elia (Viterbo), for instance, there are many gravestones from the thirties with strange, tall, thin capitals with an upside-down *N*, rectangular *U*, and an *S* with ornamental serifs. And in certain smaller cemeteries in the Marche (I have in mind the one in Giampietro and that in Monastero, in the province of Macerata), there are tombs with inscriptions in crude capitals, badly designed and fashioned even worse, with carved guiding lines and dashes separating the words. Examples in the cemetery of Montefortino (Ascoli Piceno) even have the name and dates of the deceased inscribed on the stone in handwriting.

In entirely different ways and contexts, the screeds of writing added to the tombs of various people famous for political or artistic reasons are exceptional also. They testify to a widespread desire to participate in mourning the deceased and to demonstrate their reverence in writing. Here I will merely mention the tomb of the singer James Douglas, known to the world as Jim Morrison (d. 1971), in the cemetery of Le Père Lachaise in Paris, which is entirely covered with the writings of his fans, and the entirely political case of the tomb of Thomas Sankara, young president of the African state of Burkina Faso, killed in a coup d'état on October 15, 1987, whose tomb was immediately covered with flowers and written messages of every type, set down on pages of exercise books and scraps of paper and addressed to the deceased by his anonymous supporters.

4.   Thus, in marginal zones, or in working-class and lower-middle-class funerary practices even in metropolitan areas, the writing of the

dead multiplies and tends to fill all the spaces available in spontaneous and highly inventive ways. In contrast, inscriptions on upper-class tombs are increasingly sober, almost as if a written record in the cemetery, apart from pure biographical data, is now considered superfluous, without readership, and in fact, futile. It has been noted elsewhere that between the end of the nineteenth century and the nineteen thirties, biographical records in the epigraphy of German cemeteries decreased from between 25 and 30 percent of the cases to a mere 5 percent. One could fairly say that, apart from the exceptional cases of the working-class and marginal sort already mentioned, it practically has vanished from funerary discourse.

Not only has writing the "great" been disappearing from cemeteries for some time now, but the representation of them also has moved elsewhere. Centuries ago, tombs were decked with sculpture of the highest order. Today, the involvement of a famous artist in the fashioning of a tomb is an altogether exceptional event. This is also true of writing; the best letter design is no longer housed in cemeteries. Only in the German-speaking area does one find splendid examples of modern graphics on funerary monuments—and they date from the twenties and thirties. More recently (1952–53) a tomb was erected in the cemetery of Freiburg for the Pascal family. Decked with a large slab inscribed in elegant, long, slender capitals, it is one of the few contemporary masterpieces of funerary graphics.

According to Jean-Didier Urbain, "at the base of the narrative decrease in the funerary text lies an important transformation in the attitudes and imagery relating to the status of the dead in Western society." This transformation is also evinced in the progressive distancing of new cemetcries from the city. In the United States, in the forefront here also, cemeteries are located as many as 30 or 50 kilometers from the cities they serve and have become strange green necropolises where any explicit reference to death, dead bodies, or physical decomposition is severely frowned upon. It is probably no accident that the single greatest contribution to funerary literature in verse this century, comes from the United States. I refer to *The Spoon River Anthology* by Edgar Lee Masters, published in book form in 1915 and inspired by the *Anthologia Palatina*. Even Masters's cemetery is invisible, because it is nonexistent, and the epitaphs it contains are confessions and short autobiographies confided by the dead. One can glimpse behind them the vague outline not so much of ancient Greek epigrams, but of that Anglo-American tradition of the country churchyard and its inscribed gravestones, now reaching its end. Again according to Urbain, "a society has the cemeteries it deserves; we have ours: they are invisible."

Invisible cemeteries are not places suited to exhibited writing, for the very purpose of exhibition, that of communication of the memory of the dead to others, has disappeared. This is the reason why in the sixties, a famous investigation into the death industry in the United States took no account of the problem of funerary writing. Clearly, it did not and does not exist for the numerous and rapacious firms who control both funerals and cemeteries, by now almost all privatized or commercial ventures.

It seems one must conclude that funerary writing has reached the end of its span and that Western society is about to abandon one of its principal and most particularized ways of recording death, one conceived almost twenty-seven hundred years ago and practiced ever since. Jean-Didier Urbain has drawn the same conclusion: "Does not the very evolution of the Western epitaph from the nineteenth century onward, with its diminishing quantity of graphics, its progressive and continual reduction, herald its imminent disappearance?" And again: "It may indeed be that at the end of this process of negation of the dead by the living lies the death of funerary writing itself: an absolute graphic 'silence.' The silence of the nonexistent." Yet that is not how it is. Writing, as we know, is not destined to disappear from our way of life and of creating culture. It is present in our world today as never before, in terms of the number of practitioners and of styles, testimonies, and techniques of production. It is very difficult to believe that mankind will abandon the written memory of its dead precisely at this moment. It is much more probable that the written record of death is changing form and location; that it is progressively abandoning cemeteries and moving into other practices; that even in the near future, other ways will be devised to remind men, through writing, of the names and lives of their dead predecessors. This does not remove the possibility that a society like ours, which cannot accept the idea of individual and collective death, will cease to remember its dead in the most memorable and reliable way, that of immortalizing, "in praesentia" or "in absentia," their names in writing.

Writing the dead will continue to exist, as the need of the living to record them will continue to exist, for it is the very essence of a historical vision of life and of the species.

Reference Matter

Notes

~~~

Preface

The quotation from Panofsky can be found in E. Panofsky, *Tomb Sculpture: Its Changing Aspects from Ancient Egypt to Bernini* (London, 1964), p. 9. The Vernant quotations comes from G. Gnoli and J.-P. Vernant, eds., *La mort, les morts dans les sociétés anciennes* (Cambridge and Paris, 1982), p. 7. That from Vovelle is in M. Vovelle, *Mourir autrefois* (Paris, 1974), p. 13. Apart from the above, works of a general character that have assisted greatly in the writing of this book are: H. s'Jacob, *Idealism and Realism: A Study of Sepulchral Symbolism* (Leiden, 1954); J. Sparrow, *Visible Words: A Study of Inscriptions in and as Books and Works of Art* (Cambridge, 1969); P. Ariès, *L'homme devant la mort* (Paris, 1977) and the same author's *Images de l'homme devant la mort* (Paris, 1983); M. Ragon, *L'espace de la mort* (Paris, 1981); *Mortality and Immortality: The Anthropology and Archaeology of Death*, ed. S. C. Humphreys and H. King (London, 1981); and M. Vovelle, *La mort et l'Occident de 1300 à nos jours* (Paris, 1983). In general, for the exhibited writing in the Italian tradition, see also A. Petrucci, *La scrittura: Ideologia e rappresentazione* (Turin, 1986).

The Tomb and Its Signs

The opening quotation comes from Ugo Foscolo, *Lezioni, articoli di critica e di polemica*, Edizione nazionale, 7 (Florence, 1933), p. 10. For the earliest periods of the practice of burial I have used T. Molleson, "The Archaeology and Anthropology of Death: What the Bones Tell Us," in *Mortality and Immortality*, pp. 15–32. See also R. Peroni, "Usi funerari e forme di organizzazione sociale nell'età del ferro," in *Necropoli e usi funerari nell'età del ferro: Studi*, ed. R. Peroni (Bari, 1981), pp. 293–303; M. Mussi, "Società dei vivi e società dei morti: Le sepolture del Paleolitico in Italia e la loro interpretazione," *Scienze dell' antiquità: Storia Archeologia Antropologia* 1 (1987): 37–53;

and M. Cipolloni-Sampò, "Manifestazioni funerarie e struttura sociale," ibid., pp. 55–119. On *tholoi* tombs, see O. Pelon, *Tholoi, tumuli, et cercles funéraires: Recherches sur les monuments funéraires de plan circulaire dans l'Egée de l'age du Bronze (IIIᵉ et IIᵉ millénaire av. J.-C.)*, Bibliothèque des Ecoles françaises d'Athènes et de Rome, 229 (Athens, 1976). In general, see Gnoli and Vernant, *La mort, les morts.* For Egypt, see A. J. Spencer, *Death in Ancient Egypt* (n.p., 1984); S. Bosticco, *Le stele egiziane*, vol. 1, *Le stele egiziane dall'antico al nuovo regno* (Rome, 1959), no. 18 and pp. 24–25, (the case of Simentwoser); vol. 2, *Le stele egiziane del Nuovo Regno* (Rome, 1965); vol. 3, *Le stele egiziane di epoca tarda* (Rome, 1972). For Mesopotamia, see J. Bottero, "Les inscriptions cunéiformes funéraires," in Gnoli and Vernant, *La mort, les morts,* pp. 373–406.

From the Sign to the Text

§1. The following have been of great assistance: A. Giuliano, *Arte greca dalle origini all'età arcaica* (Milan, 1986); L. H. Jeffery, "The Inscribed Gravestones of Archaic Attica," *Annual of the British School at Athens* 57 (1962): 115–53, as well as the same author's *The Local Scripts of Archaic Greece: A Study of the Origin of the Greek Alphabet and its Development from the Eighth to the Fifth Centuries* B.C. (Oxford 1961); and naturally, M. Guarducci, *Epigrafia greca*, 4 vols. (Rome, 1967–78); abridged edition: *L'epigrafia greca dalle origini al tardo Impero* (Rome 1987). A workmanlike and intelligent introduction to Greek funerary epigraphy can be found in S. Nicosia, *Il segno e la memoria: Iscrizioni funebri della Grecia antica* (Palermo, 1922), pp. 9–38. For Phoenician influences on the origins of the phenomenon, see ibid., pp. 9–11.

§2. The quotation from Vernant is in the introduction to Gnoli and Vernant, *La mort,* p. 11. The Thera epigraphs are given in Guarducci, *Epigrafia*, 1: 351, fig. 180; 1: 352–53, figs. 181a–b; 2: 392–93, figs. 123a–123b; 3: 177–78 and fig. 70; the epigraph from Corcyra is from, ibid., 2: 171 and fig. 42; Jeffery *The Local,* p. 232; that of Deinias, ibid., plate 18 (6); that of Deidamas is in Amorgo, ibid., p. 293, plate 56 (15); the Athenian epigraph of Enialo and Keramos is from, ibid., plate 2 (8) and Jeffery, "The Inscribed Gravestones," no. 22; the one from Methana is in Guarducci, *Epigrafia* , 1: 362–63 and figs. 189a–b.

§3. The stele of Dermis and Kittilos is in G. M. A. Richter, *The Archaic Gravestones of Attica* (London, 1961), figs. 31–33, 192–95, and pp. 155–56; that of Praxiteles is in Jeffery, *The Local,* plate 32, no. 3; Guarducci, *Epigrafia,* 1: 364. The stele of Holaie is in G. Bonfante and L. Bonfante, *Lingua e cultura degli Etruschi* (Rome, 1985), pp. 69–71. For the funerary art of the Etruscans, see M. Cristofani, *L'arte degli Etruschi: Produzione e consumo* (Turin, 1978). The stele of Avile Tite is in ibid., plate 110; for other Etruscan examples, see

Bonfante and Bonfante, *Lingua*, pp. 140–43. For the Warrior of Capestrano, see A. Morandi, *Epigrafia italica* (Rome, 1982), pp. 70–71 and plate 12, 1.

The Order of the Text

§1. The following have proved useful generally: William V. Harris, *Ancient Literacy* (Cambridge, Mass., 1989), in particular pp. 49–64); R. Thomas, *Oral Tradition and Written Record in Classical Athens* (Cambridge, 1989; D. Musti, "Democrazia e scrittura," *Writing and Civilization* 10 (1986): 21–48. See also C. W. Clairmont, *Gravestone and Epigram: Greek Memorials from the Archaic and Classical Period* (Mainz, 1970); J. Svenbro, *La parole et le marbre: Aux origines de la poétique grecque* (Lund, 1976); D. C. Kurtz and J. Boardmann, *Greek Burial Customs* (London, 1971); N. Loraux, *L'invention d'Athènes: Histoire de l'oration funèbre dans la "cité classique"* (Paris 1981); S. C. Humphreys, *The Family, Women, and Death; Comparative Studies* (London, 1983); C. W. Clairmont, *Patrios Nomos: Public Burial in Athens During the Fifth and Fourth Centuries* B.C.; *The Archaeological, Epigraphic-Literary, and Historical Evidence* (Oxford, 1983); J. Fedak, *Monumental Tombs of the Hellenistic Ages: A Study of Selected Tombs from the Pre-Classical to the Early Imperial Era* (Toronto, 1990); G. Hoffman, *La jeune fille, le pouvoir, et la mort dans l'Athène classique* (Paris, 1992).

As sources of reproductions, apart from Guarducci, *Epigrafia*, I have used A. C. L. Conze, *Die attische Grabreliefs* (Berlin, 1893–1922); O. Kern, *Inscriptiones Grecae* (Bonn, 1913); J. Kirchner, *Imagines inscriptionum Atticarum: Ein Bilderatlas epigraphischer Denkmäler Attikas*, 2d ed., ed. G. Klaffenbach (Berlin, 1948).

The papyrus of Timotheus (reproduced by many) can be found in W. Schubart, *Griechische Palaeographie* (Munich, 1925; reprint, 1966) pp. 98–100. The base of the stele of Teticos is in Jeffery, "The Inscribed Gravestones," no. 34; that of Chairedemos, ibid., no. 2; the stele of Pythagoras is in Guarducci, *Epigrafia*, 2: 171–72; the stele of Filo and Megakles is in Clairmont, *Gravestone and Epigram*, no. 1, plate 1; that of Kroisos is in ibid., no. 2, plate 2; the stele of Phrasikleia is in Guarducci, *Epigrafia*, 3: 124 and 3: 125; see also Jeffery, "The Inscribed Gravestones," no. 46, and J. Svenbro, *Phrasikleia: Anthropologie de la lecture en Grèce ancienne* (Paris, 1988), pp. 13–31. For the stelae of Agathon and Aristokrates, see Clairmont, *Gravestone and Epigram*, no. 66, plate 3; for the Rhodian stele of Charonidas, see Guarducci, *Epigrafia*, 1: 332–33; that of Agatocles to Archeos of Melos is in ibid., 1: 325–26; and also S. Morison, *Politics and Script: Aspects of Authority and Freedom in the Development of Graeco-Latin Script from the Sixth Century* B.C. *to the Twentieth Century* A.D., ed. N. Barker (Oxford, 1972), p. 6.

§2. For writing in democratic Athens, see in particular Musti, *Democrazia*.

The reference to Pausanias is in *Guida della Grecia*, vol. 1, *Attica*, ed. D. Musti and L. Beschi (n.p., 1982) 2–29, 16; that to Thucydides is in *La guerre du Peloponnèse: Livre II*, ed. J. de Romilly (Paris, 1962), paragraph 34. A view of the Cerameicus is in Guarducci, *Epigrafia*, 3: 130, fig. 54; the quotation from Musti is in *Democrazia*, p. 41; that from Morison is in *Politics and Script*, pp. 5–6.

§3. The stele of Eupheros is in Kurtz and Boardmann, *Greek Burial Customs*, plate 30 and pp. 130–31; that of Egheso is in Panofsky, *Tomb Sculpture*, fig. 43 and in Conze, *Die attische Grabreliefs*, vol. 1, plate 30; that of Democleides is in Panofsky, *Tomb Sculpture*, fig. 58; Guarducci, *Epigrafia*, 3: 398–99 and fig. 128; that of Ampharetes is in Kirchner, *Imagines*, plate 17, n. 38; Clairmont, *Gravestone and Epigram*, no. 23, plate 2; that of Dexileos is in Kirchner, *Imagines*, plate 21, no. 43; Guarducci, *Epigrafia*, 3: 174 and 3: 175; the contemporary stele from the Corinthian War is in ibid., 2: 168–69. For the stele of the fallen, see Musti, *Democrazia*, plate 1a; Guarducci, *Epigrafia*, 2: 164–67. The reference to Plato is to *Laws*, 12.

The Order of Memory

§1. For reproductions of Roman epigraphs I have made use of the following three collections: A. E. Gordon and J. S. Gordon, *Album of Dated Latin Inscriptions*, vol. 1, *Rome and Neighborhood: Augustus to Nerva* (Berkeley, 1958); vol. 2, A.D. *100–199* (Berkeley, 1964); vol. 2, A.D. *200–525* (Berkeley, 1965); vol. 4, *Indexes* (Berkeley, 1965); A. Degrassi, *Inscriptiones lattinae liberae rei publicae: Imagines* (Berolini, 1965); G. Walser, *Römische Inschriftkunst: Römische Inschriften für den akademischen Unterricht und als Einführung in die lateinische Epigraphik* (Stuttgart, 1988). Citations in the text refer to the *Corpus inscriptionum latinarum* (Berolini, 1861–).

In general, see I. Calabi Limentani, *Epigrafia latina*, 4th ed. (Milan, 1991), pp. 177–220; G. Susini, *Epigrafia romana* (Rome, 1982), pp. 99–110; A. Brelich, *Aspetti della morte nelle iscrizioni sepolcrali dell'impero romano*, Dissertationes Pannonicae 1, 7 (Budapest 1937); F. V. M. Cumont, *Recherches sur le symbolisme funéraire des Romains* (Paris, 1942); J. M. C. Toynbee, *Death and Burial in the Roman World* (London, 1971). The introduction by L. Bacchielli to the Italian translation, *Morte e sepoltura nel mondo romano* (Rome, 1993), contains various interesting observations. E. Weber, "Zur Enstehung der lateinischen Grabinschriften," in *Acta Colloqui Epigraphici latini*, Commentationes Humanarum Litterarum, 104 (Helsinki, 1995), pp. 253–61.

For the tomb of the Scipios, see. F. Coarelli, "Il sepolcro degli Scipioni," *Dialoghi di Archeologia* 7 (1972): 36–106; that of Lucius Scipio Barbatus is in Degrassi, *Inscriptiones*, no. 132; the quotation from Pliny the Elder comes from *Naturalis Historia* 7, 187; the tomb of Gnaeus Scipio Hispanus is in Degrassi, *Inscriptiones*, no. 137.

§2. The quotation from Pliny the Younger comes from *Epistolae* 2, 7, 7; the second quotation from Pliny the Elder is in *Naturalis Historia*, 34, 17. The monument of Caius Poplicius Bibulus is in Gordon and Gordon, *Album*, no. 2; Degrassi, *Inscriptiones*, no. 156. For the monument of Lucius Munatius Plancus, see R. Fellmann, *Das Grab des Lucius Munatius Plancus bei Gaeta* (Basel, 1957). The tombstones of Potitus Valerius Messalla, of Agrippina the Elder, of Nimphodotos, and of Sextus Varius Marcellus are in Gordon and Gordon, *Album*, nos. 14, 79, 112, 274. The cippus of Vettius Agorius Praetextatus is in Walser, *Römische Inschriftkunst*, no. 20.

§3. The quotation from Paul comes from *Iulii Pauli Sententiarum libri* 5, 1, 21, 8. That from Brelich is in *Aspetti*, p. 71.

§4. The tombs of the Isola Sacra are in Toynbee, *Death*, pp. 87, 101–3; the amphorae of the Appian Way are in Degrassi, *Inscriptiones*, nos. 314 a–c. For the mausoleum of Marcus Vergilius Eurysaces, see ibid., no. 305; P. Ciancio Rossetto, *Il sepolcro del fornaio Marco Vergilio Eurisace a Porta Maggiore*, I monumenti romani, 5 (Rome, 1973). For the funerary monument of Lucius Avillius Dionisius, see D. E. E. Kleiner, *Roman Imperial Funerary Altars with Portraits*, Archaeologica 62, no. 13 (Rome, 1987); for the stele of Publius Longidienus, see G. A. Mansuelli, *Le stele romane del territorio ravennate e del basso Po: Inquadramento storico e catalogo* (Ravenna, 1967), pp. 24–26, 102–3, 125–27, and plates 7–10.

§5. The stele of Marcus Braetius is in Walser, *Römische Inschriftkunst*, no. 81. For the inscriptions from the necropolis of the Isola Sacra of Porto, see H. Tylander, *Inscriptions du Port d'Ostie* I, II, Acta Instituti romani regni Sueciae, octavo (Lund, 1956), 4: 1–2, nos. A8 and A82. For the graphic aspect of the inscription of the two boys, Torquatianus and Lelianus, see V. De Donato, "'Pupus Torquatianus': Considerazioni sulla paleografia delle iscrizioni," *Bullettino del' "Archivio paleografico italiano"*, 3d series, 10 (1962): 7–14 (with reproduction).

The Names and the Crosses

§1. For this chapter in general, I have found particularly useful O. Marucchi, *Epigrafia cristiana: Trattato elementare con una silloge di antiche iscrizioni cristiane principalmente di Roma* (Milan, 1910); C. M. Kauffmann, *Handbuch der altchristlichen Epigraphik* (Freiburg im Breisgau, 1917); F. Grossi Gondi, *Trattato di epigrafia cristiana latina e greca del mondo romano occidentale*, I monumenti Christian dei primi secoli, 1 (Rome, 1920) ; C. Carletti, "'Epigrafia cristiana,' 'epigrafia dei Cristiani': Alle origini della terza età dell'epigrafia," in *La terza età dell'epigrafia*, ed. A. Donati, Colloquio AIEGL-Borghesi, 86 (Faenza, 1988), pp. 115–35. For the Roman situation in general see M. Guarducci, *I graffiti sotto la confessione di S. Pietro in Vaticano*, 3 vols.

(Vatican City, 1958); P. Testini, *Le catacombe e gli antichi cimiteri cristiani in Roma* (Bologna, 1966); J. Janssens, *Vita e morte del cristiano negli epitaffi di Roma anteriori al secolo VII*, Analecta Gregoriana, 223 (Rome, 1981); C. Carletti, *Iscrizioni cristiane a Roma: Testimonianze di vita cristiana (secoli III–VII)* (Florence, 1986); the text of the epitaph of Filumena is in ibid., no. 9, pp. 35–36. See also the corpus of the *Inscriptiones christianae Urbis Romae septimo saeculo antiquiores*, new series, vols. 1–9 (Rome, then Vatican City, 1922–85). The reference is to the second volume, which contains an album of photographic plates.

§2. For the reduction of names, see P. Saint-Roch, "Enquête 'sociologique' sur le cimetière dit 'coemeterium sanctorum Marci et Marceliani Damasique,'" *Rivista di archeologia cristiana* 59 (1983): 411–23. For so-called "archaic laconicism," see Carletti, "'Epigrafia cristiana,'" p. 130. The examples of figured Christian epigraphs come from Guarducci, *I graffiti*, 1: 61, fig. 2; 1: 207, fig. 83; 1: 208, fig. 84; 1: 210–11, fig. 86; 1: 395, fig. 201; *Inscriptiones christianae Urbis Romae septimo saeculo antiquiores*, no. 1723; Guarducci, *I graffiti*, 1: 287–89, fig. 250; *Inscriptiones christianae Urbis Romae septimo saeculo antiquiores*, no. 1622; C. M. Kauffmann, *Die Sepulcralen Jenseitsdenkmäler der Antike und des Urchristentums* (Mainz, 1900), fig. 2.

§3. For the graffiti of wall "g", see. Guarducci, *I graffiti*. For those of San Sebastiano, see P. Styger, "Il monumento apostolico della Via Appia," *Dissertazioni della pontificia Accademia romana di archeologia*, 2d series, 13 (1918), pp. 48–89 and plates 1–25; R. Marichal, "La date des graffiti de Saint-Sebastien," *Comptes-rendus de l'Académie des Inscriptions et Belles Lettres* (1953): 60–68; and the same author's "La date des graffiti de la Triclia de Saint-Sebastien et leur place dans l'histoire de l'écriture latine," *Revue des sciences religieuses* 36 (1962): 115–54; A. Petrucci, "Nuove osservazioni sulle origini della B minuscola nella scrittura romana," *Bullettino del' "Archivio paleografico italiano,"* 3d series, 2–3 (1963–64), pp. 65–68. For the so-called "privileged" burials, see *L'inhumation privilegiée du IVe au VIIIe siècle en Occident*, Actes du colloque tenu à Creteil les 16–18 mars 1984, ed. Y. Duval and J.-Ch. Picard (Paris, 1986); Y. Duval, *Auprès des saints corps et âmes: L'inhumation "ad sanctos" dans la chrétienté d'Orient et d'Occident du IIIe au VIIe siècle* (Paris, 1988). The formulas of closeness are in H. Leclerq, in *Dictionnaire d'archéologie chrétienne et de liturgie* 1: 1 (Paris, 1909), cols. 490, 493. The synthesis by P. Brown, *The Cult of the Saints* (Chicago, 1981), is particularly suggestive.

§4. For Christian epigraphy in Africa, see in general, V. Saxer, *Morts, martyrs, reliques en Afrique chrétienne aux premiers siècles* (Paris, 1980); P. A. Fevrier, "Evolution des formes de l'écrit en Afrique du Nord à la fin de l'antiquité et durant le haut Moyen Age," in *Tardo antico e alto medioevo: La forma artistica nel passaggio dall'antichità al medioevo*, Accademia Nazionale dei Lincei, Problemi attuali di scienza e cultura, notebook no. 105 (Rome, 1968), pp.

202–17 (the quotation on p. 207); N. Duval,"L'épigraphie funéraire chrétienne d'Afrique: Traditions et ruptures, constantes et diversités," in Donati, ed., *La terza età*, pp. 265–314. For Haïdra, see N. Duval, *Recherches archéologiques à Haïdra*, vol. 1, *Les inscriptions chrétiennes*, Collection de l'Ecole française de Rome, 18 (Rome, 1975), pp. 191–208; Y. Duval, *Loca sanctorum Africae: Le culte des martyres en Afrique du IVe au VIIe siècle*, vol. 1 (Rome, 1982), figs. 75–76; the two epitaphs are quoted in Duval, *Recherches*, no. 3, 1: 25–27 and nos. 121–22, 1: 155–58, but the interpretation of the abbreviation "MG" as "magister" remains doubtful. The epigraphs of Ain-Zara are in S. Aurigemma, *L' "area" cemeteriale cristiana di Ain-Zara presso Tripoli di Barberia*, Studi di antichità cristiana, 5 (Rome, 1935); for En-Ngila, see Fevrier, *Evolution*, pp. 209–11.

§5. For Damasine epigraphy, see A. Ferrua, *Epigrammata damasiana*, Sussidi allo studio delle antichità cristiane, 2 (Vatican City, 1942). For the imperial edict, see Saxer, *Morts*, p. 239. The episode of Sidonius Apollinaris is in the same author's *Lettres, Livres, I–V*, ed. A. Loyen (Paris, 1970), pp. 100–103. The Roman epigraphs are in A. Petrucci, "L'onciale romana: Origini, sviluppo, e diffusione di una stilizzazione grafica altomedievale," sec. 6–9, *Studi medievali*, 3d series, 12, 1 (1971): 83 and plates 2 and 3; and in G. B. De Rossi, *Inscriptiones christianae Urbis Romae septimo saeculo antiquiores*, vol. 1 (Rome, 1857–61), nos. 1119 and 1122; that of the priest Marea is in Marucchi, *Epigrafia*, pp. 421–22, n. 455; that of Eugenius can be found in a reproduction, ibid., plate 21 (and no. 457, pp. 424–26). The epitaph of Gregory the Great is in H. Grisar, *Analecta romana: Dissertazioni, testi, monumenti dell'arte riguardanti principalmente la storia di Roma e dei papi nel medio evo*, vol. 1 (Rome, 1899), plates 2, 5; for a graphic analysis, see Petrucci, "L'onciale,", pp. 84–85.

Writing the Great

§1. The opening quotation comes from by A. Thiery, "Problemi dell'arte e della cultura in Europa nei secoli VI–VIII," in *La civiltà dei Longobardi in Europa*, Accademia Nazionale dei Lincei, Problemi attuali di scienza e cultura, notebook no. 189; Atti del convegno internazionale, Rome, 1974, pp. 407–31, in particular, p. 420. The capitular of 813 is in *M. G. H.: Capitularia regum Francorum*, ed., A. Boretius, vol. 1 (Hanover, 1883), p. 174. The text of Theodulf is in E. Raunié, *Epitaphier du vieux Paris*, vol. 1 (Paris, 1890), pp. x–xi. There is mention of burials of sovereigns and their kin in churches and monasteries in *Die Urkunden der Karolinger*, vol. 1., *Die Urkunden Pippins, Karlmanns, und Karl des Grossen*, ed. A. Dopsch, J. Lechner, M. Tangl, and E. Mühlbacher (Berlin, 1956), *M. G. H.: Diplomata Karolinorum*, vol. 1, pp. 39, 49, 297, 378. My inspection of the *Corpus des inscriptions de la France médiévale* covered the first thirteen volumes (Poitiers, then Paris, 1975–88). The passage from the *Liber in gloria confessorum* of Gregory of Tours is in *M. G. H.: Scriptores rerum merovingicarum*, vol. 1 (Hanover, 1885), p. 769. The epitaphs of Venantius Fortunatus are in *M. G. H.: Auctores antiquissimi* vol. 4, 1, ed. F. Leo (Berolini, 1881), pp. 79–100. The epigraph of Ennodius is in P. Rugo, *Le iscrizioni dei secoli VI–VII–VIII esistenti in Italia* vol. 5, *La Neustria* (Cittadella, 1980), no. 130, p. 110, plate p. 226; G. Panazza, "Lapidi e sculture paleocristiane e pre-romaniche di Pavia," in *Arte del I Millennio*, Atti del II convegno per lo studio dell'arte del alto medioevo . . . (Turin, 1953), p. 230, no. 6; for that of bishop Agrippinus, see Rugo, *Le iscrizioni*, vol. 5, no. 97, pp. 89–90 and the plate on p. 208. In general, for episcopal burials in Italy, see J.-Ch. Picard, *Le souvenir des évêques: Sépultures, listes épiscopales, et culte des évêques en Italie du Nord des origines au Xe siècle*, Bibliothèque des Ecoles françaises d'Athènes et de Rome, 268 (Rome, 1988).

§2. For Merovingian funerary inscriptions in general, see E. Salin, *La civilisation mérovingienne: D'après les sépultures, les textes, et le laboratoire*, vol. 2, *Les sépultures* (Paris, 1952). The epitaph of Boetius is in J. Baum, *La sculpture figurale en Europe à l'époque mérovingienne* (Paris, 1937), plate 72, 190; that of Trasemirus is in Salin, *La civilisation*, pp. 87–88 and fig. 44; there also, pp. 144–45 and fig. 77, are the epitaph of Saint Theodechildes and that of Bertesindis and Raudoald, pp. 86–87, also in W. Boppert, *Die frühchristlichen Inschriften des Mittelrheingebietes* (Mainz, 1971), pp. 26–30; the epitaph of Bernard is in *Corpus des inscriptions de la France médiévale*, vol. 7 (Paris, 1982), pp. 76–77 and plate 21, 43. For the epigraph of Gaudiris, see S. Casartelli Novelli, "L'immagine della croce nella scultura longobarda e nell'entrelacs carolingio della diocesi di Torino," in *Riforma religiosa e arti nell'epoca carolingia*, ed. A. A. Schmid (Bologna, 1983), pp. 109–15.

§3. For the three Milanese epigraphs, in general, see A. M. Romanini, "Problemi di scultura e plastica altomedievali," in *Artigianato e tecnica nella società dell'alto medioevo occidentale*, vol. 2 (Spoleto, 1971), pp. 425–67, and in particular, pp. 450–61; Rugo, *Le iscrizioni*, vol. 5, no. 16, p. 32 and the plate on p. 159; no. 19, p. 34 and the plate on p. 162; no. 21, p. 36 and the plate on p. 163; S. Lusardi Siena, " 'Pium [su]per am[nem] iter . . . ': Riflessioni sull'epigrafe di Aldo da S. Giovanni in Conca a Milano," *Arte medievale*, 2d series, 4, no. 1 (1990): 1–12. For early medieval Italian epigraphy in general, see N. Gray, "The Palaeography of Latin Inscriptions in the Eighth, Ninth, and Tenth Centuries in Italy, *Papers of the British School at Rome* 16 (1948): 38–170, and for Lombard epigraphy proper, also see L. Capo, "Paolo diacono e il problema della cultura nell'Italia longobarda," in *Longobardia*, ed. S. Gasparri and P. Cammarosano (Udine, 1990), pp. 169–235, in particular pp. 214–16. The epitaph of Regintruda is in Panazza, "Lapidi,", no. 77, pp. 265–66 and plate 116; Gray, "Palaeography, pp. 75–76, n. 44; Capo, "Paolo," plate on p. 212;

the epitaph of Cunicperga is in Panazza, "Lapidi," pp. 263–64, n. 75 and plate III; Gray, "Palaeography, no. 45, p. 76, plate 13, 3; Capo, "Paolo," p. 232; that of Duke Audoaldus is in Panazza, "Lapidi," no. 80, pp. 267–68 and plate 110; Gray, "Palaeography, no. 46, pp. 76–77; Rugo, *Le iscrizioni*, vol. 5, no. 107, p. 97 and the plate on p. 215; Capo, "Paolo," p. 217; that of Bishop Cumianus is in Rugo, *Le iscrizioni*, vol. 5, no. 137, p. 116 and the plate on p. 229; that of the Bishop Vitalianus is in *Le iscrizioni*, vol. 3, *Esarcato, Pentapoli, e Tuscia* (Cittadella, 1976), no. 75, p. 61 and the plate on p. 122.

§4. For the epitaph of Hadrian I, see A. Petrucci, "Aspetti simbolici delle testimonianze scritte," in *Simboli e simbologia nell'alto medioevo*, vol. 2 (Spoleto, 1976), pp. 818–20 and fig. 1. For that of Paul the Levite, see Gray, "Palaeography, no. 13, p. 54 (and p. 48); for that of Pope Nicholas I, see ibid., no. 82, p. 102 and plate 20, 1; for that of Demetrius, see ibid., no. 86, plate 19, 3. For Lombard epigraphy in southern Italy, see C. Russo Mailler, *Il senso medievale della morte nei carmi epitaffici dell'Italia meridionale fra VI e XI secolo* (Naples, 1981). The epitaph of Chisa is in Rugo, *Le iscrizioni*, vol. 4, *I ducati di Spoleto e Benevento* (Cittadella, 1978), no. 56, p. 56 and the plate on p. 137; that of Prince Radelgarius is in Gray, "Palaeography, no. 121, pp. 127–28.

§5. For northern epigraphy, see S. B. F. Jansson, *The Runes of Sweden* (London, 1962), which reproduces the epitaph of Vaemod, pp. 11–15 and fig. 4, and that of Gumar, pp. 52–53 and fig. 22. The two funerary monuments from Jutland are in Baum, *La sculpture*, plate 53. Further examples can be found in ibid., plates 47, 48, 51, 52, 56. See also C. Cucina, "Modelli e caratteri di eroicità nelle iscrizioni runiche della Scandinavia vichinga," in *La funzione dell'eroe germanico: Storicità, metafora, paradigma*, ed. T. Parioli (Rome, 1995), pp. 105–40, with a recent bibliography and reproductions.

The Books and the Stones

§1. For the earliest examples, see H. Leclerq, s.v. "obituaire," in *Dictionnaire d'archéologie chrétienne et de liturgie*, vol. 12, (Paris, 1935), cols. 1834–57. For the Barberini diptych, see the same author, s.v. "diptyques," ibid., vol. 4 (Paris, 1916), cols. 1156–61; J. Vezin, "Une nouvelle lecture de la liste de noms copiés au dos de l'ivoire Barberini," *Bulletin archéologique du Comité des travaux historiques et scientifiques*, new series, 7 (1971): 19–56. The Parenzo graffiti are reproduced in P. Rugo, *Le iscrizioni dei secoli VI–VII–VIII esistenti in Italia*, vol. 2, *Venezia e Istria* (Cittadella, 1975), pp. 65–96 and plates 85–139; for the altar at Reichenau-Niederzell, see *Die Altarplatte von Reichenau-Niederzell*, ed. D. Geunich, R. Neumüllers-Klauser, and K. Schmid, Monumenta Germaniae Historica, Libri memoriales et necrologia, new series, 1; supplement (Hanover, 1983).

§2. For necrologies and obituaries in book form I have based what follows in general on J. Leclerq, "Documents sur la mort des moines," *Revue Mabillon* 65 (1955): 165–80 and *Revue Mabillon* 66 (1956): 65–81; N. Huyghebaert, *Les documents nécrologiques*, Typologie des sources du Moyen Age occidental (Turnhout, 1972), fasc. 4 A VI A I; H. Houben, "La realtà sociale medievale nello specchio delle fonti commemorative," *Quaderni medievali* 13 (1982): 82–97; J.-L. Lemaître, "Un livre vivant, l'obituaire," in *Le livre au Moyen Age*, ed. J. Glenisson (Paris, 1988), pp. 92–94. A bibliography: J.-L. Lemaître, "La commémoration des défunts et les obituaires dans l'Occident chrétien: Bulletin critique," *Revue d'histoire de l'Eglise de France* 71 (1985): 131–45. For analogous practices in the memorialization of the lay confraternity in the late Middle Ages, see J. R. Banker, *Death in the Community: Memorialization and Confraternities in an Italian Commune in the late Middle Ages* (Athens and London, 1988).

§3. For the *Liber Memorialis* of Remiremont, see G. Tellenbach, "Uno dei piú singolari libri del mondo: Il manoscritto 10 della Biblioteca Angelica in Roma (Liber Memorialis di Remiremont)," *Archivio della Società romana di storia patria* 91 (1968): 29–43; an edition with facsimiles is in *Liber memorialis von Remiremont*, 2 vols., ed. G. Tellenbach, E. Hladwitschka, and K. Schmid, Monumenta Germaniae Historica, Libri memoriales et necrologia, new series, book 1 (Dublin and Zürich, 1970) . For the necrologies of southern Italy, see M. Inguanez, *I necrologi cassinesi*, vol. 1, *Il necrologio del cod. Cassinese 47*, Fonti per la storia d'Italia, 83 (Rome, 1941); A. Garufi, "L'obituario della chiesa di S. Spirito conservato nella Biblioteca capitolare di Benevento, cod. no. 28," *Bullettino dell'Istituto storico italiano* 28 (1906): 111–24; M. Galante, "Un necrologio e le sue scritture: Salerno, sec. XI–XV," *Scrittura e Civiltà* 13 (1989): 49–328.

§4. For the so-called rolls of the dead, see. L. Delisle, *Rouleaux des morts du IXe au XVe siècle* (Paris, 1866); idem, *Rouleau mortuaire du B. Vital de Savigny contenant 207 titres écrits en 1122–1123 dans différentes églises de France et d'Angleterre* (Paris, 1909); H. Leclerq, s.v. "rouleaux des morts," in *Dictionnaire d'archéologie chrétienne et de liturgie*, vol. 12 (Paris, 1935), cols. 44–49; L. Kern, "Sur les rouleaux des morts," *Schweizer Beiträge zur allgemeine Geschichte* 14 (1956): 139–47, reprinted in the same author's *Etudes d'histoire ecclésiastique et de diplomatique* (Lausanne, 1973), pp. 99–110; J. Dufour, "Les rouleaux et encycliques mortuaires de Catalogne (1008–1102)," *Cahiers de civilisation médiévale* 20, no. 1 (January–March 1977): 13–48; the same author's, "Les rouleaux des morts," in *Codicologica*, vol. 3., *Essais typologiques* (Leiden, 1980), pp.96–102; J.-C. Kahn, *Les moines messagers: La religion, le pouvoir, et la science saisis par les rouleaux des morts, XIe–XIIe siècles* (Paris, 1987).

§5. The quotation from Mâle occurs in *L'art religieux de la fin du Moyen Age en France: Etude sur l'iconographie du Moyen Age et sur ses sources d'inspira-*

tion (Paris, 1922), p .393. The well-known tomb of Isarn of Marseilles has been repeatedly reproduced: see *Corpus des inscriptions de la France médiévale*, vol. 14 (Paris, 1989), no. 55 and plate 31, fig. 63; B. Rupprecht, *Romanische Skulptur in Frankreich* (Munich, 1975), plate 10; A. Erlande-Brandenburg, *Le roi est mort: Etude sur les funérailles, les sépultures, et les tombeaux des rois de France jusqu'à la fin du XIIIᵉ siècle*, Bibliothèque de la société française d'archéologie, 7 (Geneva, 1975), pp. 110–11. The tombstone of Sancho of Navarre and Castile is in F. A. Greenhill, *Incised Effigial Slabs: A Study of Engraved Stone Memorials in Latin Christendom, c. 1100 to 1700*, 2 vols. (London 1976), no. 100b. The tombstone of Rudolph of Sweden is in K. Bauch, "Anfänge des figürlichen Grabmals in Italien," *Mitteilungen des Kunsthistorischen Instituts in Florenz* 15 (1971): 243 and fig. 18; that of E. de Fouilly is in A. Michel, *Histoire de l'art depuis les premiers temps chrétiens jusqu'à nos jours*, vol. 2, 1 (Paris, 1906), p. 191 and fig. 152; the tombs of Jean and of Blanche de France are in Erlande-Brandenburg, *Le roi est mort*, plate 29. For Italy, see B. Breveglieri, *Scrittura e immagine: Le lastre terragne del medioevo bolognese* (Spoleto, 1993). An imaginary reading of tomb inscriptions appears in Chrétien de Troyes, *Le Chevalier de la Charette*, ed. M. Roques (Paris, 1958), pp. 57–59, lines 1849–1909.

Monument and Document

§1. The Latin text of Boncompagno is in the Vatican Library, ms Arch. S. Pietro H 13, ff.45v–46r; I am acquainted with two editions, both largely incorrect: F. Burger, *Geschichte der florentinischen Grabmals von den ältesten Zeiten bis Michelangelo* (Strasbourg, 1904), p. 21, and I. Herklotz, *"Sepulcra" e "monumenta" del medioevo: Studi sull'arte sepolcrale in Italia*, Collana di studi di storia dell'arte, 5 (Rome, 1985), p. 239. The Milanese monument of Oldrado da Tressena in A. Petrucci, "Mille anni di forme grafiche nell'area milanese," in *Il millennio ambrosiano: La nuova città dal comune alla signoria*, ed. C. Bertelli (Milan, 1989), pp. 140–63, in particular p. 151, fig. 182, and p. 160.

§2. The quotation from Krautheimer comes from *Roma: Profilo di una città, 312–1308* (Rome, 1981), p. 255; that from Herklotz, whose work remains fundamental for the documentation of the overall phenomenon, occurs in *"Sepulcra,"* p. 193.

§3. For the works of the "Rome marble masons," see P. C. Claussen, *Magistri doctissimi romani: Die römischen Marmorkünstler des Mittelalter* (Stuttgart, 1987). For the funerary monuments and work in Rome of Arnolfo di Cambio, see (to cite only the most recent bibliography) J. Osborne, "The Tomb of Alfanus in S. Maria in Cosmedin, Rome, and Its Place in the Tradition of Roman Funerary Monuments," *Papers of the British School at Rome* 51 (1983), pp. 240–48; A. M. Romanini, *Arnolfo di Cambio e lo "stil novo" del gotico italiano* (Milan, 1969); more particularly, A. M. D'Achille, "Sulla datazione del monumento funebre di Clemente IV a Viterbo: Un riesame delle fonti," *Arte medievale*, 2d series, 3 no. 2, (1989), pp. 85–91; the same author's "Il monumento funebre di Clemente IV in S. Francesco a Viterbo," in *Skulptur und Grabmal des Spätmittelalters in Rom und Italien*, ed. J. Garms and A. M. Romanini, Akten des Kongresses "Scultura e monumento sepolcrale del tardo medioevo a Roma e in Italia," Rome, July 4–6, 1985, (Vienna, 1990), pp. 192–242; A. M. Romanini, "Ipotesi ricostruttive per i monumenti sepolcrali di Arnolfo di Cambio," ibid., pp. 107–28; and S. Romano, "Giovanni di Cosma," ibid., pp. 159–71. For artists' signatures, see Petrucci, *La scrittura*, pp. 11–12 and especially P. C. Claussen, "Früher Künstlerstolz: Mittelalterliche Signaturen als Quelle der Kunstsoziologie," in *Bauwerk und Bildwerk im Hochmittelalter* (Giessen, 1981), pp. 7–34.

§4. For the Scaligeri funerary monuments, see F. De Maffei, *Le arche scaligere di Verona* (Verona, 1955); K. Bauch, *Das mittelalterliche Grabbild: Figürliche Gräbmäler des 11. bis 15. Jahrhunderts in Europa* (Berlin and New York, 1976), pp. 189–91; for the monument of Henry VII, see ibid., p. 172, fig. 274; for that of Bishop Ubertini, see ibid., pp. 178–79; for that of Sanseverino, see F. Negri Arnoldi, "Sulla paternità di un ignoto monumento campano e di un noto sepolcro bolognese," in *Skulptur und Grabmal*, pp. 431–38. For more in general, see also *Niveo de marmore: L'uso artistico del marmo di Carrara dall'XI al XV secolo*, ed. E. Castelnuovo (Genoa, 1992.)

§5. The quotation from J. Le Goff refers to the entry s.v. "documento/ monumento," in *Enciclopedia*, vol. 5 (Turin, 1978), pp. 38–48.

The Body, Knowledge, and Money

§1. For the figure of the late medieval university professor, see. J. Le Goff, *Les intellectuels au Moyen Age*, 2d ed., (Paris, 1985). For the monuments of the Bolognese professors, see C. Ricci, *Monumenti sepolcrali di lettori dello Studio bolognese* (Bologna, 1886); R. Grandi, *I monumenti dei dottori e la scultura a Bologna (1267–1348)* (Bologna, 1982); the same author's "Dottori, scultori, pittori: Ancora sui monumenti bolognesi," in *Skulptur und Grabmal*, pp. 353–65; G. Sanders, "La pérennité du message épigraphique: De la communauté chrétienne élitaire du Bas-Empire au corps professoral de l'université médiévale de Bologne," in *La terza età dell'epigrafia*, pp. 349–414. The quotation from Riccobaldo da Ferrara can be found in L. A. Muratori, *Rerum italicarum scriptores*, vol. 9 (Mediolani, 1726), col. 133. For the earliest epitaphs of Guglielmo da Lucca and of Giovanni Bassiano, see B. Breveglieri, *Scritture lapidarie romaniche e gotiche a Bologna: Osservazioni paleografiche in margine alle iscrizioni medievali bolognesi* (Bologna, 1986), plates 3 and 4, pp. 16–24. The sale document of August 28, 1372 with the description of the scholar's tombstone, pointed out to me by Paola Supino Martini, is in *Chartularium Studii Bononiensis: Documenti per la storia dell'Università di Bologna dalle origini al secolo XV*, vol. 4 (Bologna, 1919), no. 188 (1114), pp. 123–24 . For a French tombstone of a *magister*, that of Guillaume de Saint-Remy, after 1340, see *Les fastes du Gothique: Le siècle de Charles V* (Paris, 1981), no. 37, pp. 93–94.

§2. On the new figure of the lay writer in Italy between the thirteenth and fifteenth centuries, see A. Petrucci, "Il libro manoscritto," in *Letteratura italiana*, ed. A. Asor Rosa, vol. 2, *Produzione e consumo* (Turin, 1983), pp. 506–22. The Morelli quotation is from Giovanni da Pagolo Morelli, *Ricordi*, ed. V. Branca (Florence, 1956), pp. 228–29; the quotation from Alberti is in L. B. Alberti, *I libri della famiglia*, ed. R. Romano and A. Tenenti (Turin, 1969), p. 251. On the so-called "family books" in general, reference is necessarily to A. Cicchetti and R. Mordenti, "La scrittura dei libri di famiglia," in *Letteratura italiana*, ed. A. Asor Rosa, vol. 3, *Le forme del testo*, part 2, *La prosa* (Turin, 1984), pp. 1117–59 and the same authors' *I libri di famiglia in Italia*, vol. 1, *Filologia e storiografia letteraria* (Rome, 1985). The following examples are used in the text : *Il libro di ricordanze dei Corsini (1361–1457)*, Fonti per la storia d'Italia, 100 (Rome, 1965), pp. 5, 82; Morelli, *Ricordi*, p. 182; the last quotation from Alberti, *I libri*, is from p. 215.

§3. On the history of pre-Humanism in Padua, see. G. Billanovich, "Il preumanesimo padovano," in *Storia della cultura veneta: Il Trecento*, vol. 2 (Vicenza, 1976), pp. 19–110, in particular, pp. 92–110; for the quotation from Lovato, see pp. 60–61; for the funerary monument of Lovato, see pp. 21–23 and plate 48; for the tomb of Rolando da Piazzola, see p. 99 and plate 51. The quotation from Petrarch is in his *De remediis utriusque fortune* (Lugduni, 1577), p. 170. For the epigraphs he composed, see A. Petrucci, *La scrittura di Francesco Petrarca*, Studi e Testi, 248 (Vatican City, 1967), pp. 68–69 and plate 20, 1 and 2. For the epigraphs of Salutati, see L. Miglio, "Un nome per tre epitaffi: Coluccio Salutati e gli elogi funebri dei Corsini," *Italia medioevale e umanistica* 26 (1983): 361–74.

Florence and Rome

§1. For the monument of John XXIII in the Florence Baptistery, see S. Black McHam, "Donatello's Tomb of Pope John XXIII," in *Life and Death in Fifteenth-Century Florence*, ed. M. Tetel, R. G. Witt, and R. Goffen, (Durham, 1989), pp. 146–73, 232–42; and also H. W. Janson, *The Sculpture of Donatello*, vol. 1 (Princeton, 1957), pp. 59–65 and plates 85–92. The bibliography on the Humanist graphic reform is very vast; here let me refer to a brilliant essay by E. H. Gombrich, "From the Revival of Letters to the Reform of the Arts: Niccolò Niccoli and Filippo Brunelleschi," in *Essays in the History of Art Presented to R. Wittkower*, vol. 2 (London, 1967), pp. 71–82; and also to M. Meiss, "Toward a More Comprehensive Renaissance Palaeography," *The Art Bulletin* 42 (1960): 97–112; E. Casamassima, *Trattati di scrittura del Cinquecento italiano* (Milan, 1966), in particular pp. 9–36; Petrucci, *La scrittura*, pp. 21–36. In general, see also S. T. Strocchia, *Death and Ritual in Renaissance Florence* (Baltimore, 1992).

§2. On the funerary oration in the Italian Renaissance, see the wide-ranging work, rich in good ideas, of J. McManamon, *Funeral Oratory and the Cultural Ideals of Italian Humanism* (Chapel Hill, 1989). For the pavement tombstone of Bishop Pecci, see Janson, *The Sculpture*, pp. 75–77 and plates 109–11b. For that of Martin V in Saint John Lateran, see ibid., pp.232–35 and plates 485–86; Panofsky, *Tomb Sculpture*, p. 72 and figs. 310–11. For the monument of Leonardo Bruni in Santa Croce, see L. H. Heydenreich and G. Passavant, *Rinascimento*, Storia della scultura nel mondo (Milan, 1980), p. 69. For the chapel of Giacomo del Portogallo, see F. Hartt, G. Corti, and C. Kennedy, *The Chapel of the Cardinal of Portugal* (Philadelphia, 1964). For the Federighi funerary monument, see R. F. von Lichtenberg, *Das Porträt an Grabdenkmalen: Seine Entstehung und Entwickelung vom Alterthum bis zum italienischen Renaissance* (Strasbourg, 1902), plate 35; J. Pope-Hennessy, *Italian Renaissance Sculpture* (London, 1958), p. 295 and plate 47.

§3. On the rebirth of the classical epigraphic capital, see G. Mardersteig, "Leon Battista Alberti e la rinascita del carattere lapidario romano nel Quattrocento, in *Italia medioevale e umanistica* 2 (1959), pp. 285–307; and, in addition to some of the works already cited, also see A. Petrucci, " 'L'antiche e le moderne carte': Imitatio e renovatio nella riforma graphic umanistica," in *Renaissance und Humanistenhandschriften* (Munich, 1988), pp. 1–12. The quotation from Alberti comes from *L'architettura: De re aedificatoria*, vol. 2, ed. G. Orlandi and P. Portoghesi (Milan, 1966), p. 965. For the tomb of Piero and Giovanni de' Medici by Verrocchio, see C. Seymour, Jr., *The Sculpture of Verrocchio* (London, 1971), pp. 161–62 and plates 33–40; Panofsky, *Tomb Sculpture*, fig. 302. For "Sistine" epigraphy in late fifteenth-century Rome, see S. Maddalo, "Il monumento funebre tra persistenze medioevali e recupero dell'antico," in *Un pontificato ed una città: Sesto IV (1471–1484)*, Littera Antiqua, 5 (Vatican City, 1986), pp. 429–52; D. Porro, "La restituzione della capitale epigrafica nella scrittura monumentale: Epitafi ed iscrizioni celebrative," ibid., pp. 409–27; Petrucci, *La scrittura*, pp. 25–28. The Roman funerary monuments of the period are reproduced and also commented on in G. S. Davies, *Renascence: The Sculptured Tombs of the XVth Century in Rome* (London, 1910). For the tomb of Sixtus IV, see L. D. Ettlinger, *Antonio and Piero Pollaiuolo: Complete Edition with a Critical Catalogue* (London, 1978), pp. 148–51 and plates 110–28. For the monument and the Sassetti Chapel, see Panofsky, *Tomb Sculpture*, p. 73 and plates 314–15, and especially A. Warburg, *Francesco Sassettis Letzwillige Verfügung, Gesammelte Schriften*, vol. 1 (Leipzig,

1932), pp. 127–63. On the funerary chapels and equestrian monuments of the Italian Renaissance in general, see W. J. Wegener, *Mortuary Chapels of Renaissance Condottieri* (Ann Arbor, 1990), and on the tomb of Colleoni, pp. 156–77; and also M. Collareta, "Ritratti, stemmi e iscrizioni: Il contributo dell'arte alla memoria dei defunti," in *Il Duomo di Trento: Pitture, arredi, e monumenti*, ed. E. Castelnuovo (Trento, 1993), pp. 63–87.

From the Stone to the Page

§1. The first quotation is taken from A. Tenenti, *Il senso della morte e l'amore della vita nel Rinascimento (Francia e Italia)* (Turin, 1957), p. 445. For *transi* tombs, see K. Cohen, *Metamorphosis of a Death Symbol: The Transi Tomb in the Late Middle Ages and the Renaissance* (Berkeley, 1973). For the tomb of Fievez, see Panofsky, *Tomb Sculpture*, p. 58, fig. 229; for that of Chichele, see Cohen, *Metamorphosis*, pp. 15–16 and fig. 13; for that of Yver, see ibid., pp. 59–60 and fig. 19; for that of Flamel, ibid., fig. 44. For tomb slabs, see in general the great, if untidy, collection by F. A. Greenhill, *Incised Effigial Slabs: A Study of Engraved Stone Memorials in Latin Christendom, c.1100 to 1700*, 2 vols. (London, 1976).

§2. For the thinking of Michelangelo, see Ch. De Tolnay, *Michelangelo*, vol. 3, *The Medici Chapel* (Princeton, 1948), fig. 90 and pp. 73–75; and also E. Panofsky, "Mors vitae testimonium: The Positive Aspect of Death in Renaissance and Baroque Iconography," in *Studien zur Toskanischen Kunst: Festschrift für L. H. Heydenreich* (Munich, 1964), pp. 231–32; M. Weinberger, *Michelangelo the Sculptor*, 2 vols. (London, 1967), vol. 1, fig. 90. For the tomb of Cecchino Bracci, see E. Steinmann, "Studien zur Renaissanceskulptur in Rom. II: Das Grabmal des Cecchino Bracci," *Monatshefte für Kunstwissenschaft* 1 (1908): 963–74; De Tolnay, *Michelangelo*, vol. 3, p. 81 and plates 124, 125, 306; the poems are in Michelangelo Buonarroti, *Rime*, ed. E. N. Girardi, Scrittori d'Italia 164 (Bari, 1960), pp. 363–79, nos. 179–228; and also the analysis by S. Matarasso-Gervais in Michel-Ange Buonarroti, *Epitaphes pour la Mort de François des Bras* (Aix-en-Provence, 1983), in particular pp. 7–75. For the tombs of Sansovino in Santa Maria del Popolo, see H. Keutner, *Sculpture: Renaissance to Baroque* (London, 1969), fig. 35; E. Bentivoglio and S. Valtieri, *Santa Maria del Popolo* (Rome, 1976), figs. 46, 47; for the monument to Bembo, see Sparrow, *Visible Words*, fig. 45; for that to Louis de Brézé, see Cohen, *Metamorphosis*, figs. 103–9; for that to Cardona, see J. M. Azcárate, *Escultura en el siglo XVI*, Ars Hispaniae: Historia universal del arte hispánico, 13 (Madrid, 1958), fig. 10; for that to the Earl of Rutland, see A. T. Friedman, "Patronage and the Production of Tombs in London and the Provinces: The Willoughby Monument of 1591," *The Antiquaries' Journal* 65 (1985): 390–401; see also the rich documentation given by M. Rossi, *La poesia sculpita: Danese Cataneo nella Venezia del Cinquecento* (Lucca, 1995), in particular pp. 104–31.

§3. For Pontano's *I tumuli* and shrine, see G. Parenti, "L'invenzione di un genere, il tumulus pontaniano," in *Interpres* 7 (1987): 125–58; J. J. Pontani, *Carmina, Ecloghe, Elegie, Liriche*, ed. J. Oeschger, Scrittori d'Italia, no. 198 (Bari, 1948), pp. 189–258; Sparrow, *Visible Words*, pp. 20–25; see ibid., pp. 25–37 for collections of inscriptions. The most complete bibliography of collections of inscriptions or of funerary texts are Parenti, *L'invenzione*, and F. S. Quadrio, *Della storia e della ragione d'ogni poesia*, vol. 2 (Milan, 1741), pp. 663–82.

§4. For Mazocchi and his three editions of epigraphs, see F. Ascarelli, *Annali tipografici di Giacomo Mazzocchi*, Biblioteca bibliografica italiana, no. 24 (Florence, 1961), no. 130, pp. 126, 128; no. 144, pp. 139–41; no. 157, p. 150. The quotation from Sannazaro is in *Opere volgari*, ed. A. Mauro, Scrittori d'Italia, no. 220 (Bari, 1961), p. 137. The first edition of Porcacchi's *Funerali antichi* mentioned in the text was published in Venice in 1574. For the *Rime di diversi nobilissimi et eccellentissimi autori in morte della signora Irene delle signore di Spilimbergo* . . . (Venice, 1561), see E. Favretti, "Una raccolta di rime del Cinquecento," *Giornale storico della letteratura Italiana* 158 (1981): 543–72; and A. Jacobson-Schutte, "Commemorators of Irene di Spilimbergo," in *Renaissance Quarterly* 45 (1992), pp. 524–35. The poem by Jean Dorat is in his *Oeuvres poétiques*, ed. C. Marty-Laveaux (Paris, 1875), pp. 45–46. The *Epitaphes* of Ronsard are in his *Oeuvres complètes*, vol. 2, ed. G. Cohen, (Paris, 1966), pp. 474–543. For Schrader's anthology, published in Helmstadt in 1592, see Sparrow, *Visible Words*, p. 27; and ibid., pp. 28–30, for the *Monumenta* of Rybisch and Fendt. The bull of Pius V is in *Bullarium diplomatum et privilegiorum sanctorum romanorum pontificum turinensis editio* . . . , vol. 7, (Turin, 1862), p. 436.

The Theaters of Pain

§1. The opening quotation comes from E. Tesauro, *Il cannocchiale aristotelico sia idea dell'arguta et ingeniosa elocutione che serve a tutta l'arte oratoria, lapidaria, et simbolica* . . . (Venice, 1663), p. 549. On Baroque epigraphy, see the observations in Petrucci, *La scrittura*, pp. 54–64. The quotation from Góngora is in Luis Góngora y Argote, *Obras completas*, ed. J. Mille y Gimenez and I. Mille y Gimenez (Madrid, 1972), sonnet 228, p. 447.

§2. For the Gaignières collection, see J. Adhémar and G. Dordon, "Les tombeaux de la collection Gaignières: Dessins d'archéologie du XVIIe siècle," *Gazette des beaux arts* 116 (1974): 3–192. For the collections of epigraphs by Weever and others, see Sparrow, *Visible Words*, pp. 25–37. The quotation on the funeral ceremony of Leo XI is taken from *Descrizione dell'esequie di n. s. p. Leone XI celebrate nel Duomo di Fiorenza il di 16 maggio 1605* (n.p., nd.); it should be noted that this ceremony is the subject of another *Descrizione dell'essequie di papa Lione XI celebrate nel Duomo di Firenze da' signori operai, d'ordine del serenissimo Gran Duca* (Florence, 1605), with remarkable variants in the transcription of the texts displayed. (Exemplars consulted: Rome, Vatican Library, p.4.63, 6 and D.5.5, 20.)

§3. The quotation from Chastel is in "Le Baroque et la Mort," in *Retorica e Barocco*, Atti del III Congresso internazionale di Studi Umanistici, ed. E. Castelli (Rome, 1955), p. 33. For funeral ceremonies, the earliest and most authoritative treatise (and collection) I know of is by the Jesuit C. F. Menestrier, *Des décorations funèbres où il est amplement traité des tentures, des lumières, des mausolées, catafalques, inscriptions, et autres ornements funèbres . . .* (Paris, 1684), with a list on pp. 19–36; the quotation is from p. 232. There is another collection by O. Berendsen, *The Italian Sixteenth and Seventeenth Century Catafalque* (New York, 1961) (thesis; exemplar consulted in the Bibliotheca Hertziana, Rome). For Charles V, see F. Checa, "Un programma imperialista: El túmulo erigiso en Alcalá de Henares en memoria de Carlos V," *Revista de Archivos, Bibliotecas, y Museos* 82, no. 2 (1979): 369–79. The record of the funeral ceremony of Michelangelo is entitled *Esequie del divino Michelangelo Buonarroti celebrate in Firenze dall'Accademia de' Pittori, Scultori et Architettori nella chiesa di San Lorenzo il di 28 Giugno MDLXIII* (Florence, 1564); that of Grand Duke Cosimo I: *Descritione della pompa funerale fatta nelle essequie del ser.mo sig. Cosimo de' Medici Gran Duca di Toscana nell'alma città di Fiorenza il giorno XVII di Maggio dell'anno MDLXXIIII* (Florence, 1574). The report of the funeral rites for the wife of Pietro of Valle was set down by Girolamo Rocchi: *Funerali della Signora Sitti Manni Gioerida della Valle moglie di Pietro della Valle* (Rome, 1627). On the phenomenon of the funeral procession, see M. Moli Frigola, "Donne, candele, lacrime, e morte: Funerali di regine spagnole dell'Italia del Seicento," in *Barocco romano e barocco italiano: Il teatro, l'effimero, l'allegoria*, ed. M. Fagiolo and M. L. Madonna (Rome, 1985), pp. 135–58; and also M. A. Visceglia, "Corpo e sepoltura nci testamenti della nobiltà napoletana (XVI–XVIII secolo)," *Quaderni storici* 50 (1982): 583–614. See also M. Rosa, "Morte e trasfigurazione di un sovrano: Due orazioni per Cosimo III," in *La Toscana nell'età di Cosimo III* (Florence, 1994), pp. 419–36.

§4. For the funerary sculptures of Bernini, see Panofsky, "Mors vitae testimonium," and Petrucci, *La scrittura*, pp. 60–61. For the Vecchiarello monument, see L. Bruhns, "Das Motiv der ewigen Anbetung in der römischen Grabplastik des 16., 17., und 18. Jahrhunderts," *Römisches Jahrbuch für Kunstgeschichte* 4 (1940), fig. 243. For the monument of Doge Pesaro, see Petrucci, *La scrittura*, p. 63 and fig. 54. For the Busby tomb, see K. A. Esdaile, *English Monumental Sculpture Since the Renaissance* (London, 1927), p. 133 and plate 13. The von Freiberg funerary monument is in A. E. Brinckmann, *Barock Skulptur: Entwicklungsgeschichte der Skulptur in der romanischen und ger-*

manzischen Ländern seit Michelangelo bis zum Beginn des 18. Jahrhunderts (Berlin, 1917), p. 350 and fig. 364. For French examples, see F. Ingersoll-Smouse, *La sculpture funéraire en France au XVIIIe siècle* (Paris, 1912), respectively pp. 17 and 42–43. For the Mordaunt monument, see Esdaile, *English Monumental Sculpture*, p. 131 and plate 8.

Anglo-Americana

§1. For the English funerary production I have used B. Willsher and D. Hunter, *Stones: A Guide to Some Remarkable Eighteenth Century Gravestones* (Edinburgh, 1978); P. Rahtz, "Artefacts of Christian Death," in *Mortality and Immortality*, pp. 117–36. The first quotation comes from J. Weever, "A Discourse of Funerall Monuments," the foreword to his *Ancient Funerall Monuments*, p. 1.

§2. For literacy in the American colonies, see H. J. Graff, *The Legacies of Literacy: Continuities and Contradictions in Western Culture and Society* (Bloomington, Ind., 1987), pp. 248–57. In general, see Vovelle, *La mort*, pp. 425–34.

§3. The diary of Joshua Hempstead has been published as: *Diary of Joshua Hempstead of New London, Connecticut, Covering a Period of Forty-Seven Years, from September, 1711 to November, 1758 . . .* (New London, Conn., 1901).

§4–5. For American funerary production between the seventeenth century and the early nineteenth century I have principally used H. M. Forbes, *Gravestones of Early New England and the Men Who Made Them: 1653–1800* (Boston, 1927); A. I. Ludwig, *Graven Images: New England Stonecarving and Its Symbols: 1650–1815* (Middletown, Conn., 1966); D. Tahshijan and A. Tahshijan, *Memorials for Children of Change: The Art of Early New England Stonecarving* (Middletown, Conn., 1974); P. Benes, *The Mask of Orthodoxy: Folk Gravestone Carving in Plymouth County, Massachusetts, 1680–1805* (Amherst, Mass., 1977); F. J. Baker, "Toward Memory and Mourning: A Study of Changing Attitudes Toward Death Between 1750 and 1850 as Revealed by Gravestones of the New Hampshire Merrimack River Valley Mourning Pictures, and Representative Writing" (Diss., The George Washington University, 1977); C. F. Swineart, *Gravestone Art: The Tombstone Cutters of Early Fairfield County, Ohio, and Their Art* 1968 (Lancaster, Ohio, 1984). For the "rural" tradition of American cemeteries from Mount Auburn (Boston, 1831) onward, see D. C. Sloane, *The Last Great Necessity: Cemeteries in American History* (Baltimore, 1991), pp. 44–64.

Ordering the Corpses, Ordering the Writing

§1. For the expulsion of tombs from churches and the establishment of cemeteries outside cities, see Vovelle, *La mort*, pp. 461–95; M. Foisil, "Les attitudes devant la mort au 18ᵉ siècle: Sépultures et suppression de sépultures dans le cimetière parisien des Saints Innocents," *Revue historique* 251, no. 510 (1974): 303–30; J. Thibaut-Payen, *Les morts, l'église, et l'état: Recherches d'histoire administrative sur les sépultures et les cimetières dans le ressort du Parlement de Paris au XVIIᵉ et XVIIIᵉ siècles* (Paris, 1977). For the Modena episode, see. M. Bulgarelli, "La riforma della sepoltura nobilare a Modena," *Studi storici* 31 (1990): 999–1015.

§2. On tomb literature, see P. Van Tieghem, *La poésie de la nuit et des tombeaux en Europe au XVIIIᵉ siècle*, Mémoires de l'Académie royale de Belgique, classe des lettres et sciences morales et politiques, 2d series, 16, fasc. 1 (Brussels, 1928); J. McManners, *Morte e illuminismo: Il senso della morte nella Francia del XVIII secolo* (Bologna, 1984), pp. 421–504.

§3. The quotation from Foscolo on English burial literature in U. Foscolo, "Lettera a Monsieur Guillon," in *Scritti letterari e politici dal 1796 al 1808*, ed. G. Gambarin, Edizione nazionale delle opere di U. Foscolo, 6 (Florence, 1972), pp. 505–49, in particular p. 518, no. 17; the second quotation is from U. Foscolo, *Saggio sulla letteratura contemporanea in Italia* in *Saggi di letteratura italiana*, vol. 2, ed. C. Foligno, Edizione nazionale delle opere di U. Foscolo, 11 (Florence, 1958), p. 549. See also L. Sozzi, "I 'Sepolcri' e le discussioni francesi sulle tombe negli anni del Direttorio e del Consolato," *Giornale storico della letteratura italiana* 144 (1967): 576–88; and R. Scarcia, *Due studi di filologia* (Rome, 1979), pp. 21–64.

§4. On Baskerville, see D. C. McMurtrie, *The Book: The Story of Printing and Bookmaking* (London, 1967), pp. 373–83 (with reproduction of the title page of the Virgil on p. 375). On Bodoni, see Petrucci, *La scrittura*, pp. 87–90. The tomb of Maurice of Saxony is in Ingersoll-Smouse, *La sculpture*, plate 11; s'Jacob, *Idealism and Realism*, plate 22b. The tomb of Ferdinand VI is in Keutner, *Sculpture*, plate 295. For Canova, apart from the article by M. Pavan in the *Dizionario biografico degli Italiani*, vol. 18 (Rome, 1975), pp. 197–219, I have mainly used A. Muñoz, *Antonio Canova: Le opere* (Rome, 1957), and F. Licht and D. Finn, *Canova* (Milan, 1984). The quotation from R. Longhi is in his *Viatico per cinque secoli di pittura veneziana* (Florence, 1946), p. 43. The quotation from Stendhal comes from his *Oeuvres intimes* (Paris, 1957), p. 1161.

§5. The initial quotation from A. Cesari comes from his *Biografie, elogj, epigrafie, memorie italiane e latine*, ed. G. Guidetti (Reggio Emilia, 1908), p.340; the other appears on p. 339. The Orioli work is entitled *Iscrizioni di autori diversi con un discorso sulla epigrafa italiana* (Bologna, 1826). Giordani's views are published in M. Ricci, *Tre lettere di Pietro Giordani sul comporre le iscrizioni volgari* (n.p., n.d.), and in A. Foratti, *Pietro Giordani epigrafista* (Padua, 1905), pp. 8–9. The collection of Giordani's inscriptions cited in the text is: P. Giordani, *Iscrizioni* (Parma, 1834). Giordani's 1813 opinion appears in his "Delle sculture ne' sepolcri: Discorso all'Accademia di Belle Arti in

Bologna, 1813," in *Scritti editi e postumi*, vol. 2., ed. A. Gussalli, II (Milan, 1856), pp. 294–302, in particular p. 294. For Manuzzi, see E. Sbertoli, "Qualche nota su una raccolta ottocentesca di epigrafi funebri," *Archivio storico italiano* 149 (1991): 663–85. I quote the Belli sonnet, dated January 23, 1833, from Belli, *I sonetti*, vol. 2, ed. G. Vigolo (Milan, 1952), no. 815, p. 1123. His views on a Milanese cemetery are also worth considering and are given in G. G. Belli, *Lettere giornali zibaldone*, ed. G. Orioli (Turin, 1962), pp. 74–75.

The Middle Class and Its Writing

§1. The quotation from Maupassant comes from G. de Maupassant, "Les tombales," in his *Contes et nouvelles*, vol. 2, ed. by L. Forestier (Paris, 1979), pp. 1239–40. Examples of graphic styles in use in European cemeteries are in R. Aloi, *Architettura funeraria moderna: Architettura monumentale, crematori, cimiteri, edicole, cappelle, tombe, stele, decorazione . . .* (Milan, 1941; reprint, 1969).

§2. For the Pellegrini cemetery, see M. Piccolo, *Cenni sul cimitero nuovo di Napoli con raccolta delle migliori iscrizioni* (Naples, 1881). I am indebted to my friend Prof. Vittorio Dini for pointing it out and making it available. For the Verano in Rome, many reproductions are in C. Cianferoni, *Cimitero del Verano in Roma: Cappelle, tombe, e lapidi* (Turin, 1915). For Staglieno, see G. Grasso and G. Pellicci, *Staglieno* (Genoa, 1974). The preface, by Corrado Maltese, is the source of the quotation from him. For Giusti's reaction, see his *Poesie edite e inedite* (Milan, 1884), pp. 121–25; the tombstone composed for him by Capponi is in Batini, *La Toscana*, p. 53. A recent work on the funerary epigraphs of the Canton Ticino is F. Soldini, *Le parole di pietra: Indagini sugli epitaffi cimiteriali otto-novecenteschi del Mendrisiotto* (Freiburg, 1990).

§3. For war cemeteries, see Vovelle, *La mort*, pp. 646–50; A. Hüppi, *Kunst und Kult der Grabstätte* (Osten, 1968), pp. 429–37; G. L. Mosse, "National Cemeteries and National Revival: The Cult of the Fallen Soldiers in Germany," *Journal of Contemporary History* 14 (1979): 120; R. Koselleck, "Les monuments aux morts: Contribution à l'étude d'une marque visuelle des temps modernes," in *Iconographie et historei des mentalités* (Paris, 1979), pp. 113–23; B. Cousin and G. Richier, "Les monuments aux morts de la guerre 1914–1918 dans les Bouches-du-Rhône," ibid., pp. 124–30; C. Canal, "La retorica della morte: I monumenti ai caduti della grande guerra," *Rivista di storia contemporanea* 11 (1982): 659–69; M. Isnenghi, *Le guerre degli Italiani: Parole, immagini, ricordi, 1848–1945* (Milan, 1989), pp. 341–49. The reproduction of the monument of the Ecole des Beaux-Arts is in M. Rheims, *La sculpture au XIXe siècle* (Paris, 1972), plate 45 and p. 335.

§4. For the Italian military cemeteries of the Great War, see the reproductions in Aloi, *Architettura*, plates 1–16; *Sacrari militari della prima guerra mondiale: Redipuglia-Oslavia (e altri sacrari del Friuli Venezia Giulia e d'oltre confine)* (Rome, 1980). The commemorative mottoes are on pp. 27 and 31. "Thoughts for the Times on War and Death" (1915) appears in Sigmund Freud, *Collected Papers,* vol. 4 (London, 1925), pp. 304 and 307. For American war cemeteries, see J. F. Marion, *Famous and Curious Cemeteries* (New York, 1977), pp. 52–74. See also G. Wills, *Lincoln at Gettysburg: The Words that Remade America* (New York, 1992), pp. 63–89.

§5. For the presence of death in the daily press, see Vovelle, *La mort,* pp. 752–53; W. Fuchs, *Le immagini della morte nella società contemporanea* (Turin, 1972), pp. 82–98. For mourning cards, see J.-D. Urbain, "Feuille de marbre et stèle volante," *Actions et recherches sociales* no. 2 (June 1990): 26–30. For nineteenth-century France, see P. Simoni, "Notices nécrologiques et élites locales: L'élite aptésienne au XIXe siècle," *Annales du Midi* 87 (1975): 67–95.

Multiply and Decrease

§1. For English mourning cards of the Victorian period, see J. Morley, *Death, Heaven, and the Victorians* (London, 1971), fig. 9.

§2. Pointers to the phenomena examined in this paragraph and the following are already to be found in Petrucci, *La scrittura,* pp. 112–13.

§3. The investigation of Calabrian tombs gave rise to an exhibition and catalog, *Imago Mortis: Simboli e rituali della morte nella cultura popolare dell'Italia meridionale,* curated by F. Faeta and M. Malabotti (Rome, 1980). Carlo Tedeschi has generously provided me with a wealth of documentation for other Italian regions.

§4. J.-D. Urbain's contributions are fundamental to the study of contemporary funerary epigraphy, in particular *L'archipel des morts: Le sentiment de la mort et les dérives de la mémoire dans les cimetières d'Occident* (Paris, 1989); the quotations in the text occur on pp. 201, 35, 208, and 210–11. German and Swiss examples of contemporary funerary epigraphy are in Aloi, *Architettura,* plates 216–54. The tomb of the Pascal family is in Hüppi, *Kunst,* pp. 481–82 and fig. 201. For the American situation, the essential references are to J. Mitford's monograph, *The American Way of Death* (New York, 1963), and to R. E. Meyer, ed. *Ethnicity and the American Cemetery* (Bowling Green, Ohio, 1993); J. G. Brown, *Soul in the Stone: Cemetery Art from America's Heartland* (Lawrence, Kans., 1994).

Index of Names

Library of Congress Cataloging-in-Publication Data

Petrucci, Armando.
 Writing the dead : death and writing strategies in the Western
tradition / Armando Petrucci ; translated by Michael Sullivan.
     p.   cm. — (Figurae)
 Includes bibliographical references and index.
   1. Epitaphs.   2. Inscriptions.   3. Sepulchral monuments.
I. Title   II. Series: Figurae (Stanford, Calif.)
CN77.P49   1998
929'.5—dc21   97-28232
                                                        CIP

Original printing 1998
Last figure below indicates year of this printing:
07   06   05   04   03   02   01   00   99   98

CPSIA information can be obtained
at www.ICGtesting.com
Printed in the USA
LVHW091922231020
669657LV00005B/35